W9-CCY-640

"Child sexual abuse is one of the most damaging and life-altering experiences a person can suffer. This workbook offers the guidance and support survivors desperately need by providing powerful exercises to help them deal with the associated emotions of shame, fear, sadness, and anger, as well as offering advice and strategies to help them cope with such issues as nightmares and flashbacks. I highly recommend it."

—**Beverly Engel, LMFT**, author of *It Wasn't Your Fault* and *The Right to Innocence*

"*The Sexual Trauma Workbook for Teen Girls* is an amazing book of *hope*, *inspiration*, and *education* from start to finish. With the sharing of different personal experiences and encouragement, this book will help any young teen at any point of their journey to recovery. As a fellow survivor of rape and sexual assault, I wish this workbook had been available for me during my time of need. Although it's been over twenty years since my rape and sexual assault, this workbook helped me today address and conquer emotions that I thought no longer existed."

—**Tanisha Bagley**, survivor of over ten years of rape, sexual assault, and domestic violence; advocate for all victims and survivors of rape, sexual assault, and domestic violence; and author of *The Price of Love*

"This practical and enlightening book is a blessing for teen girls and the adults who support them following sexual trauma. It is filled with research-based wisdom, everyday tools, guidance, and most of all, hope!"

—**Marilyn Price-Mitchell, PhD**, developmental psychologist and author of *Tomorrow's Change Makers*

"In *The Sexual Trauma Workbook for Teen Girls*, the authors have done a beautiful job of providing a wise, inspiring, uplifting, and comprehensive guide for healing, which can be used alone or as an adjunct to therapy. I love this book. It is comforting and practical, and I will recommend it often."

—**Catherine McCall, MS, LMFT**, author of the international best seller *Never Tell*, is on the judges panel of the United Kingdom Child Sexual Abuse People's Tribunal, RAINN Speakers Bureau, and a blogger for *Psychology Today*

# the sexual trauma workbook for teen girls

## a guide to recovery from sexual assault & abuse

RAYCHELLE CASSADA LOHMANN, MS, LPC
SHEELA RAJA, PhD

Instant Help Books
An Imprint of New Harbinger Publications, Inc.

Publisher's Note

*This publication is designed to provide accurate and authoritative information in regard to the subject matter covered. It is sold with the understanding that the publisher is not engaged in rendering psychological, financial, legal, or other professional services. If expert assistance or counseling is needed, the services of a competent professional should be sought.*

Distributed in Canada by Raincoast Books

Copyright © 2016 by Raychelle Cassada Lohmann and Sheela Raja

Instant Help Books
An Imprint of New Harbinger Publications, Inc.
5674 Shattuck Avenue
Oakland, CA 94609
www.newharbinger.com

Cover design by Amy Shoup

Acquired by Tesilya Hanauer

Edited by Gretel Hakanson

All Rights Reserved

Library of Congress Cataloging-in-Publication Data on file

18 17 16

10 9 8 7 6 5 4 3 2 1 First Printing

R0445684916

This book is dedicated to the many strong women who shared parts of their story to help those, who like themselves, are survivors of sexual trauma. This book is also dedicated to Regan, whose inspiring story helped make this book become a reality.

To my wonderful husband, son, and daughter, your gracious support and love encourages me to follow my dreams and fulfill my passion to help others.

~Raychelle Cassada Lohmann

This book is dedicated to the countless women and girls who have trusted me enough to allow me to be a part of their journey toward healing. Your kindness, intellect, and strength are an endless source of inspiration and hope.

Thank you to my husband, daughters, and sister for their unwavering support, and love. Words cannot express my gratitude for my husband, who shares a commitment to making the world safer and more peaceful for our daughters. His wisdom means everything to me. I am deeply indebted to my parents, Vasantha and Raja, who model compassion, support, empathy, and forgiveness every single day. And thank you to every woman who has been a role model in my life, including my aunts Saroja and Reena and my second-grade teacher Cynthia Miller Webb, who understood the importance of seeing the potential in every child.

~Sheela Raja

# Contents

# letter from the authors

Dear Reader,

First let us begin by saying *thank you. Thank you* for being brave enough to open this book and begin the first step to recovery. *Thank you* for trusting us to teach you skills you can use in your everyday life to cope with your thoughts, feelings, and emotions. Most of all *thank you* for allowing us to be a part of your healing journey.

Just by working through this book, you are showing bravery and courage to face your anger, fears, insecurities, and shame, and we promise we won't take that for granted. We will guide you down this difficult yet rewarding path as you learn to stand strong and move from being a sexual trauma victim to a survivor, a survivor who can grow from your traumatic experience(s). You don't have to let your past define who you are, but rather let it shape you into the courageous young woman you are destined to become.

As you walk through the contents of this workbook, you will be asked to explore some tough experiences that you may shy away from. You will be asked to face emotions that you may otherwise run from. There may be times when you think, *I can't do this,* but you can. It is our sincere goal to compassionately guide you every step of the way. You are not alone. We will sequentially teach you skills to apply to your everyday life, making you feel more confident and secure to take the next step. When you see that you have the strength to move forward, you will feel more empowered to do it again and again.

We do ask that if you ever feel as though life is unbearable or hopeless or if you have thoughts of hurting and harming yourself, then you should get help immediately. Also, if there are things you are doing that are interfering with healing, such as drinking, taking drugs, or exposing yourself to risky or dangerous situations, then you should seek help immediately. Do not wait to get help. People care about you and want to help you through this difficult time. If you are unsure if you need more help, the book contains many exercises and questions to help you make that decision.

This workbook should be used as a healing guide; it is not our intent for it to replace counseling. Rather it would be beneficial to use this workbook in conjunction with therapy.

This journey is your journey, and no one's story is like yours. Along with friends, family, and professional support, we hope this book will provide you with the tools you need to recover and live the life you truly want.

Empowering you with confidence and success,

Raychelle Cassada Lohmann and Sheela Raja

# knowing when to get help 1

## you need to know

In this book we use the terms *sexual trauma* and *sexual abuse* to describe many types of experiences. These may be single incidents, or they may have continued over time. Sexual trauma may involve rape or inappropriate sexual touching, or you may have felt pressured to perform certain sexual acts out of fear. Not all sexual violation involves the use of physical force, but the survivor often feels ashamed, fearful, angry, and helpless both during and after the incident.

## my story

*I felt so isolated after the rape. I remember how numb I felt, as if I were watching myself from outside of my body. I felt like no one really could understand what I was going through. The only thing I wanted to do was sleep. I couldn't eat and lost about twenty pounds in a very short amount of time. I knew I couldn't go on like this, and my family and friends had no idea how to help me. I was angry and distant. I needed someone who knew how to hold my pain and help me navigate through it without getting overwhelmed. For me, that meant finding the right therapist, the right medication, and the right people to be around.* ~Emily

You may feel that the sexual trauma you have experienced is too much to handle on your own. Perhaps you aren't sure whether or not you need more help. You might feel that if you ask people for help, they will think you are weak, or maybe you're too embarrassed to talk about sex with an adult. These feelings are completely normal. Opening up to a stranger isn't easy, but there are trained professionals who can help you get through this hurtful experience.

Counselors are trained to help you work through your painful experiences at a comfortable pace. Most importantly, they can teach you coping skills and help you manage hurtful thoughts and emotions. These skills will help you grow into a more confident and stronger woman.

# directions

Review the checklist below and check any symptom that applies to you.

## Therapy Needs Checklist

### Coping

- ☐ I engage in risky and unhealthy behaviors, such as having unprotected sex, drinking alcohol, or taking drugs.
- ☐ I have recently gained or lost a lot of weight.
- ☐ I frequently withhold food from myself even though I haven't eaten much.
- ☐ I have episodes where I vomit after eating, exercise excessively, or use laxatives or other extreme means to prevent weight gain.

### Daily Activities

- ☐ I worry so much that it interferes with my daily activities (for example, or going to school, going to work, or being with friends).

### Emotions

- ☐ I feel sad most of the time.
- ☐ I no longer enjoy doing the things I use to.
- ☐ I am angry most of the time.
- ☐ I often feel like there is no hope.
- ☐ I often feel out of control of my moods.

## Relationships

- ☐ I am in a relationship that is emotionally, physically, or sexually abusive.
- ☐ I feel like people come and go from my life, and I don't have lasting friendships.
- ☐ I have a difficult time trusting people.
- ☐ I worry so much about what others think of me that I am unable to make or keep friends.

## Thoughts of Hurting Yourself

- ☐ I have recurrent thoughts of death, dying, and suicide.
- ☐ I have tried to hurt myself by cutting, burning, or engaging in other kinds of behavior that could seriously injure me.
- ☐ I have attempted or threatened suicide.

## Trauma Memories

- ☐ Memories of my sexual trauma are interfering with my daily life (for example, concentrating at school, or getting along with others).
- ☐ I worry that memories about my sexual trauma might overwhelm me.
- ☐ I have frequent nightmares about the sexual event.
- ☐ When something reminds me of my sexual trauma, I sometimes feel I am reliving what happened to me.
- ☐ I experience physical symptoms, such as difficulty breathing, dizziness, or racing heartbeat, when I think about what I experienced.
- ☐ I have periods of time where I feel disconnected from reality.
- ☐ I spend a lot of time and energy avoiding people and places that remind me of the event.

Number of marked responses: ________

If you checked any of the statements regarding suicidal thoughts, self-injurious behavior, drug use, or alcohol use, please get help immediately. If you are currently in a relationship that is abusive, please reach out for help. And if you checked any of the statements, please consider getting professional help. People care about you and want to help. If you are working with a therapist, please take this activity to your next session and speak with your therapist about your answers.

# more to do

There are many benefits to speaking with a professional about your experience(s).

Counseling can help you

- feel better about yourself
- cope with your past
- feel more connected to others
- decrease stress and anxiety
- reclaim personal control and power

Answer the following questions.

1. If you aren't in therapy, what is keeping you from giving it a try? For example, are you afraid of talking about the event, or are you ashamed of what happened?

______________________________

______________________________

______________________________

2. If you didn't have to worry about what you listed above, how could therapy help you?

______________________________

______________________________

______________________________

3. If you are currently seeing a professional, what things are you learning that help you better cope with your past?

4. If you aren't in therapy and are trying to find a trained sexual abuse professional, start by reaching out to your local rape crisis center (where confidential counseling is often provided free or at very low cost). The staff can help you locate a counselor and answer your questions. List the name and contact information of your local center below.

## words of inspiration

*You are worthy of love and care and healing. Find people who lift you up.* ~Emily

# 2 where to find help

## you need to know

When you have experienced sexual trauma, you may feel helpless, frightened, and scared. You may not know who or where to turn to for help. Fortunately, there are many organizations that are specifically designed to help sexual abuse survivors find help and support, and nurture each other as they heal.

## my story

*From the nurses to the investigators, I met so many people in the hospital. I believe these people were the first step in my process to finding the help that I would need moving forward. They offered the understanding and support that I needed. I remember the officers handed me a card for the local rape crisis center. And within a few short days of my incident, I was sitting in a circle of women who all had a story similar to mine. I was scared that I would have to tell everyone what had happened to me and that it would be hard to talk in a group setting, but in all actuality the group of women were exactly the strength I needed to be able to tell my story.* ~Regan

Many sexual abuse organizations offer a variety of resources, such as helping you find

- a trained sexual trauma therapist in your area
- a sexual abuse support group so you can connect with others
- a safe place to stay, if you are in danger
- an attorney who specializes in sexual trauma to help you determine whether or not you want to take legal action

If you haven't already, please take time to become familiar with the organization(s) in your area and seek their assistance.

# directions

Explore the sexual abuse agencies where you live. If you aren't sure where to start, try searching online for "rape victim resources" or "sexual assault support groups." There is also a resource list at the end of the book that lists organizations that are devoted to raising sexual abuse awareness and advocating for your rights.

List the name and contact information for each facility in your area.

# more to do

List three things your local agencies could help you with (such as finding a support group or someone to reach out to in difficult times).

1. ______________________________

______________________________

______________________________

2. ______________________________

______________________________

______________________________

3. ______________________________

______________________________

______________________________

# words of inspiration

*Words are your power to heal, and the louder you speak, the more you can heal.* ~Regan

# 3 personal safety plan

## you need to know

Your safety should always come first. One way to help you feel safe is to develop a personal safety plan. A safety plan is a personalized blueprint that helps you identify places, things, and people that help you cope with the journey ahead.

## my story

*When I was thirteen, I met my boyfriend at his cousin's house. Our plan was to meet there before heading to the state fair with our friends. When I went upstairs to use the bathroom before leaving, his nineteen-year-old cousin sexually assaulted me on the bathroom floor. It happened so fast. As I began to heal and started to socialize again, I developed my own personal safety plan as a strategy to suppress my fears and to feel comforted. My plan included the buddy system. I made sure that if I was going to someone's house, I knew exactly who would be there. I also knew what I would do if I found myself in danger again. Having a plan helped me feel less like a victim and more confident and secure.* ~Amanda

As a survivor of sexual abuse, you have been robbed of something that others take for granted—the feeling of safety. During the course of this book, you will be asked to explore some sensitive, uncomfortable, and painful experiences. It's important that you have a safety plan in place where you identify people, places, and things to help you cope as you begin the road to recovery.

Safety plans include identifying people, places, things, and resources.

- People that you trust, such as family, friends, teachers, coaches, or counselors: If you aren't sure if you can trust them, think about how they have reacted in the past when you or someone else has gone through a difficult time. Have they shown understanding and warmth? If so, these are people that you may be able to trust.

- Places where you spend a lot of time, such as home, school, and work: Have safety zones at these places where you can go if you feel emotionally overwhelmed or fear you're in danger. For example, at home do you feel safest in your room, in the family room, or when you are around other people? At school do you feel comfortable going to the counselor's office or a favorite teacher's room during his or her planning period?

- Things you can do or surround yourself with to feel more secure: For example, do you have a favorite childhood stuffed animal, a picture that holds fond memories, or a sentimental trinket that soothes you when you're upset? Do you do something that helps you cope, such as listen to music, write, draw, play a game, or read?

- Resources you will need for your plan: For example, will you need your phone to reach a friend or family member? Will you need a buddy system to have friend to walk you to and from classes? Will having a soothing item such as an inspirational quote or a sentimental trinket help you feel calmer and more hopeful during your most difficult moments?

# directions

You are the only one who knows what "feeling safe" means to you. You can design your personalized safety plan below to make sure you feel safe and secure.

## Personal Safety Plan

Name: ______________________________________________

### Home

How safe do I feel at home on a scale of 1 to 10? __________
(1 = not at all safe. 10 = completely safe.)

Places at home where I feel more secure (for example, my room, or the kitchen): ______

______________________________________________

People I can reach out to when I don't feel safe at home: ______________________

______________________________________________

What I can do when I feel unsafe at home: ______________________________

______________________________________________

Things that can soothe me at home: ______________________________

______________________________________________

Resources I need to feel safe at home: ______________________________

______________________________________________

## School

How safe do I feel at school on a scale of 1 to 10? ____________
(1 = not at all safe. 10 = completely safe.)

Places I feel safe at school: ______________________________

______________________________

People I can reach out to when I don't feel safe at school: ______________________________

______________________________

What I can do when I feel unsafe at school: ______________________________

______________________________

Things that can soothe me at school: ______________________________

______________________________

Resources I need to feel safe at school: ______________________________

______________________________

Other Location: ________________________________________ (such as work)

How safe do I feel at ____________ on a scale of 1 to 10? ____________
(1 = not at all safe. 10 = completely safe.)

Places I feel safe at this location: ______________________________________

______________________________________________________________________

People I can reach out to when I don't feel safe in this setting: ______________

______________________________________________________________________

What I can do when I feel unsafe at this setting: ________________________

______________________________________________________________________

Things that can soothe me at this setting: ______________________________

______________________________________________________________________

Resources I need to feel safe in this setting: ____________________________

______________________________________________________________________

## more to do

Once you complete your personal safety plan, place it where you can access it easily. You may want to consider making copies and giving them to the people you listed on your plan. Be sure to share your safety plan with your therapist.

## words of inspiration

*It is possible to give and receive love in healthy relationships after you experience a sexual assault. Develop a safety plan and a healing plan, and stick to it.* ~Amanda

# 4 circle of support

## you need to know

We all need people in our life to help us get through good and bad times. Depending on our situation, we may rely on friends, family members, teachers, and other people that we know and trust. We seek these people out for various reasons, and they form our circle of support.

## my story

*Right after the incident, the first person I wanted was my mom because she gave me comfort, support, and unconditional love. While Mom was amazing, I quickly realized I needed someone who had gone through this before and came out okay on the other side. I desperately needed to talk to a survivor, someone who could truly understand what I was going through. I found this person and many others in a rape crisis support group. This group was made up of people who were like me, people who could identify with my experience. It was comforting to go into a room with these people, my friends, and feel like I wasn't crazy. I was surrounded by people who knew exactly what I was going through and didn't judge me. These people formed my circle of support, and I don't know where I'd be today without them.* ~Regan

A circle of support is a network of people who play different roles in your life, such as friend, confidant, caretaker, advocate, and so on. They are the people who are there during life's good and bad times. They push you to achieve your dreams, celebrate your accomplishments, and provide you with support during difficult times.

There are two parts to your support circle: the inner circle and the outer circle.

## *The Inner Circle*

Your inner circle is comprised of the people whom you can be the "real you" around and whom you connect with emotionally. These people accept you for who you are. Some have a lot of people in their inner circle, but most have only a few. Either way it's okay. The important thing is that you have someone you trust and can turn to during tough times.

Inner circle people

- care and love you unconditionally
- encourage you to keep persevering, even when you want to give up
- lift you up when you're feeling down
- believe in your ability to get through tough times
- listen and understand what you're going through

## *The Outer Circle*

Your outer circle is made up of casual friends. These are people that you enjoy being around and going places with, but you may not tell them everything. They are the friends who may let you borrow a textbook if you forgot yours, loan you money for lunch, or give you a ride when you need one. They aren't as close as your inner circle, but they still play an important role in your life.

Outer circle people

- help with day-to-day things
- are fun to be around
- boost your mood when you're sad
- treat you with kindness and respect

# directions

Who is in your circle of support? Complete each ring of the circle with the following information:

**You:** Write what you need most from your support circle. For example, do you need people who will listen, understand what you're going through, and believe in you?

**Inner Circle:** Write the names of the people whom you reach out to the most. Who are you closest to in life? Who supports you during the hard times? Who celebrates your successes with you?

**Outer Circle:** Write the names of the people who are casual friends. These are the people whom you enjoy talking to, spending time with, and being around.

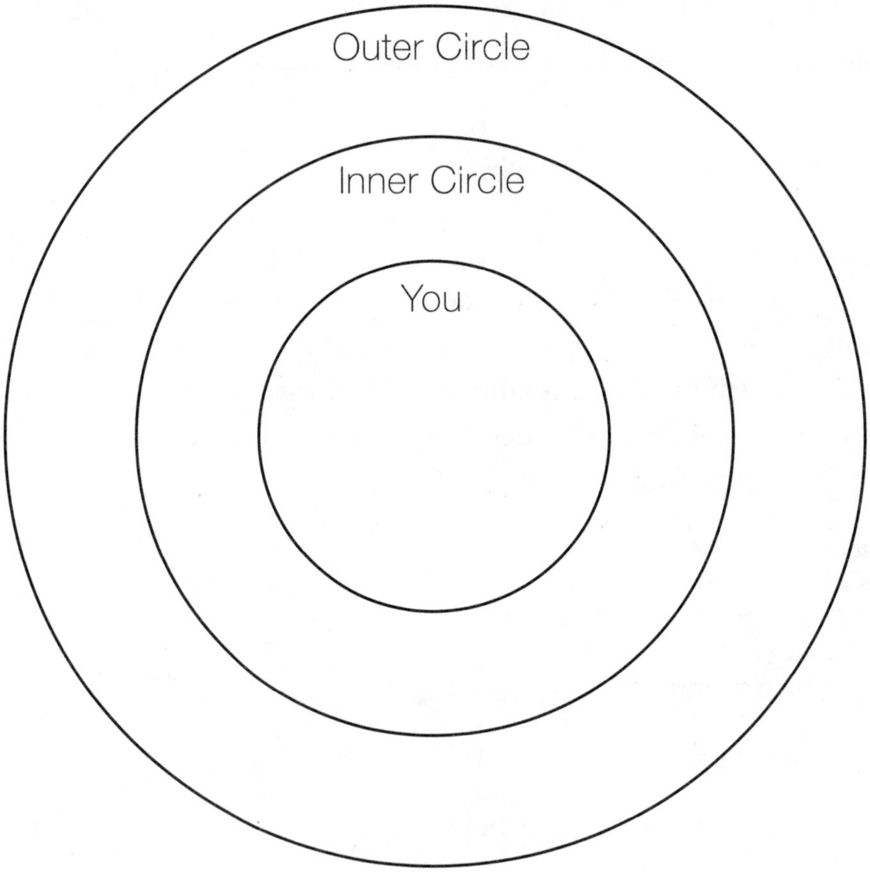

# more to do

You chose the people in your circles for a reason, probably because each person fulfills a personal need. What *personal need* does each person in your circles meet?

| Inner Circle | | |
|---|---|---|
| Person's Name | Why I Choose This Person | Why I Need This Person |
| Aubrey | best friend since childhood | I trust her, and she is always there for me. |
| | | |
| | | |
| | | |
| | | |
| | | |

| Outer Circle | | |
|---|---|---|
| Person's Name | Why I Choose This Person | Why I Need This Person |
| | | |
| | | |
| | | |
| | | |
| | | |

# words of inspiration

*You don't ever have to feel like you're alone because there are people that love you and understand what you are going through. All you have to do is identify them.* ~Regan

# why me? 5

## you need to know

It's natural for survivors to ask the question, why me? over and over again. Unfortunately, there isn't a clear answer to this question. In truth, it's never acceptable for a person to sexually violate someone else, and you did nothing wrong. In life, bad things happen to good people, and this is especially true for survivors of sexual assault. Part of healing is learning to find ways to deal with the question, why me? and still live the life you want.

## my story

*Following the sexual abuse, I would ask myself, Why me? Over time I realized it was because I was the youngest, most vulnerable, and easiest to target. Did that knowledge help me cope with the reality that I was going to be dealing with this for the rest of my life? Not really. However, over time I have developed a strength that has grown exponentially within me. This strength has prepared me to take on whatever comes my way. I learned I was strong and would not let him or the sexual abuse hold me back. I may have felt powerless at the time of the incident, but I have since refused to relinquish that power to the person who harmed me. I no longer ask,* Why me? *I know why. The experience has helped me evolve into the strong, independent woman that I am today. It has made me a compassionate, tolerant, and dependable person for those in need. It gave me the curiosity to explore human behavior and the drive to put myself through school and earn a degree from a prestigious university. It has given me the determination for the relentless pursuit of success and happiness.* ~Jessica

Ruminating is the act of focusing on pain and replaying this type of question over and over again. Although asking yourself questions like "Why me?" and "What did I do wrong?" is perfectly normal, when it keeps you stuck and overwhelmed, it is unhelpful. Overcoming ruminating involves the following:

- Identifying the thoughts you play repeatedly in your mind, like *Why me?* or *What did I do wrong?*
- Understanding how ruminating affects you. For example, do you get depressed, panicky, or angry?
- Taking the power away from those thoughts by telling yourself, *I don't know why this happened to me, but I'm not going to let it keep me from having moments of happiness.*
- Allowing ruminating thoughts to freely come and go. Don't hold on to them and don't let them keep you down.

# directions

Work through the strategies below to stop ruminating thoughts.

1. What unhelpful thoughts do you play repeatedly in your mind?

 ________________________________________________

 ________________________________________________

 ________________________________________________

 ________________________________________________

2. How does ruminating on these thoughts affect you? For example, do you feel depressed, anxious, or angry?

 ________________________________________________

 ________________________________________________

 ________________________________________________

 ________________________________________________

3. Look at the thoughts you listed in question 1, and insert each one into the statement below.

 I am having the thought that ______________________________.
 It's perfectly normal for me to have these kinds of thoughts. Having these thoughts doesn't mean that I can't pay attention to what I'm doing today or what's going on in this moment.

 Practice this statement each time you start to ruminate on a thought.

4. Recognize that your thoughts can freely come and go. Have you ever watched clouds float in the sky? Some are big, some are small, some are bold and dark, some move fast, and some move slow. Thoughts are a lot like clouds. Some pass by quickly, and some linger. Just like clouds, thoughts will eventually float away. For each thought that you previously listed, imagine it being attached to a cloud and let it freely float away at its own pace.

5. Pay attention to what is happening right here and now. Listen to the sounds of nature or focus on the colors that surround you. Write the good things going on in your life; whether they're big or small, they matter. For example, did you get a part in a play, are you planning something fun with some friends, or are you into a TV series that you can't wait to see the next episode of?

______________________________________________

______________________________________________

______________________________________________

______________________________________________

# more to do

The next time you find yourself ruminating on a thought, write it down and practice one of the strategies listed above until you are able to break the cycle.

# words of inspiration

*Don't let what happened to you define you as a person in a negative way. Be determined to turn it into a positive. As difficult as they may be, the bad things that happen make us stronger and wiser. We can use that strength and wisdom to help others, which can be super healing!* ~Jessica

# 6 sharing your story

## you need to know

No two individuals share the same life story, and that's what makes us so unique. Our stories are made up of pleasant and unpleasant memories, happy and painful experiences, and secure as well as insecure beliefs about ourselves. Whether you have been the victim of date rape, molested by a family member or friend, or assaulted by a stranger, you may find healing in sharing your story. While you may not feel ready to share your story with a lot of people, there is one person you need to be honest and open with...*yourself*.

## my story

*I was assaulted during the same attack as my college roommate. We both shared the same date of attack, location, and even some of the same memories; however, what each of us took out of the attack was unique. In fact, I am not sure to this day, almost fifteen years later, that we have ever discussed with each other the events of that night. What I do know is that when I look back on the attack, I know would not change a single thing about how I handled it. There were times during the incident that each of us could have made a decision other than the one that we made, but the reality is, at the time, we were not going to leave the other one behind. I will always be grateful for my friend for choosing to make the same decision I did and not leave me even though she could have.* ~Gabby

Interwoven in the activities of this book are vignettes from sexual abuse survivors. These women wanted to share a part of their story with you with the hope that you could use their story to help you gain courage, peace, and strength. Many of these women have traveled a path similar to yours. Although everyone is different, many survivors experience common emotions, thoughts, and feelings. The survivors in this book know what it takes to survive sexual assault, and they want to pass this knowledge on to you so you too can find peace in your story.

## directions

Sharing your story may not be easy, especially if this is the first time that you've acknowledged the event(s) you experienced. Also, if you don't feel ready to share your entire story, don't force yourself. And make sure you have support if you need it. With time, you'll be ready to share more and more of it. At your own pace, begin writing your story in the space below.

## my story

## more to do

Just like the women in this book, you too can find strength in your story. At the end of each activity, you may have noticed that these women left you with words of inspiration. Take a look at your story and leave yourself with some words of inspiration.

My words of inspiration:

______________________________________________________________

______________________________________________________________

______________________________________________________________

## words of inspiration

*You are strong. Reach deep down and find strength and power in your story.* ~Gabby

# taking care of yourself 7

## you need to know

Taking good care of yourself may be a challenge when you have survived sexual abuse. When your world has been turned upside down, things that were once easy may now seem difficult and complicated. Even though you may not feel like taking care of yourself, it is an essential part of your recovery.

## my story

*Learning how to "deal" in healthy ways was really difficult after the rape. It was hard to eat, much less eat the right kinds of foods. It was hard to exercise. It was hard to find people who understood how much pain I was in and were willing to deal with my distant behavior and random spells of crying. It took some time to regain my footing on life and realize that if I didn't take care of myself, no one else would. I journaled my feelings. I forced myself to eat. I forced myself to go for walks, even when I didn't feel like it. And slowly, gradually, I began to feel like I was going to make it through.* ~Emily

Taking care of yourself involves nurturing and balancing three parts of your well-being: your mind, body, and spirit.

## *Your Mind*

Your mind generates your thoughts and gives you messages about life. At times, some of these thoughts may be painful and untrue. For example, you may think that you deserved what happened or that you are "dirty" or "tainted." Your mind can be very stubborn. It can tell you that things are impossible, or you may end up believing your thoughts are 100 percent accurate. It's useful to examine a thought from all angles and think about alternative ways to look at the situation. For example, if you find yourself thinking, *This experience has made me used and dirty*, an alternate way to look at it is, *One experience does not define who I am. I am not the one who is at fault.*

## *Your Body*

The body is the vessel that allows you to get up and function each day. Just like a flower needs soil, nutrients, water, and sun to survive, your body needs regular exercise (thirty minutes of moderate activity per day), sleep (eight to ten hours per night), nutritious food, and relationships to survive. Your body depends on you to take care of it so it will bloom and thrive. To care for your body, start with small goals like taking a walk twice a week or replacing an afternoon candy bar with a piece of fruit.

## *Your Spirit*

The spirit is difficult to describe because it's the part of you that goes beyond your mind and body. It is the core of your existence, encompassing your views, your personality, and the things that you are passionate about. There are many ways you can charge your spirit. Some people find yoga, religious practices, and meditation help feed their soul, which in turn positively influences their mind and body. Others find that soothing music or the smell of their favorite candle can be centering and meaningful.

In order to care for yourself, you must find a balance between the mind, body, and spirit. All three components are interconnected, and a weakness in one will create an imbalance in another.

# directions

Do you have balance in your body, mind, and spirit?

In each circle, list things that balance and nourish your well-being. For example, in the mind circle, write a painful thought and challenge it by asking if it is 100 percent accurate. In the body circle, write how can you meet your physical needs (for example, exercise three times a week or reduce your intake of caffeinated and sugary drinks). In the spirit circle, write down how you can nurture your spirit (for example, a walk in nature or volunteer to help others).

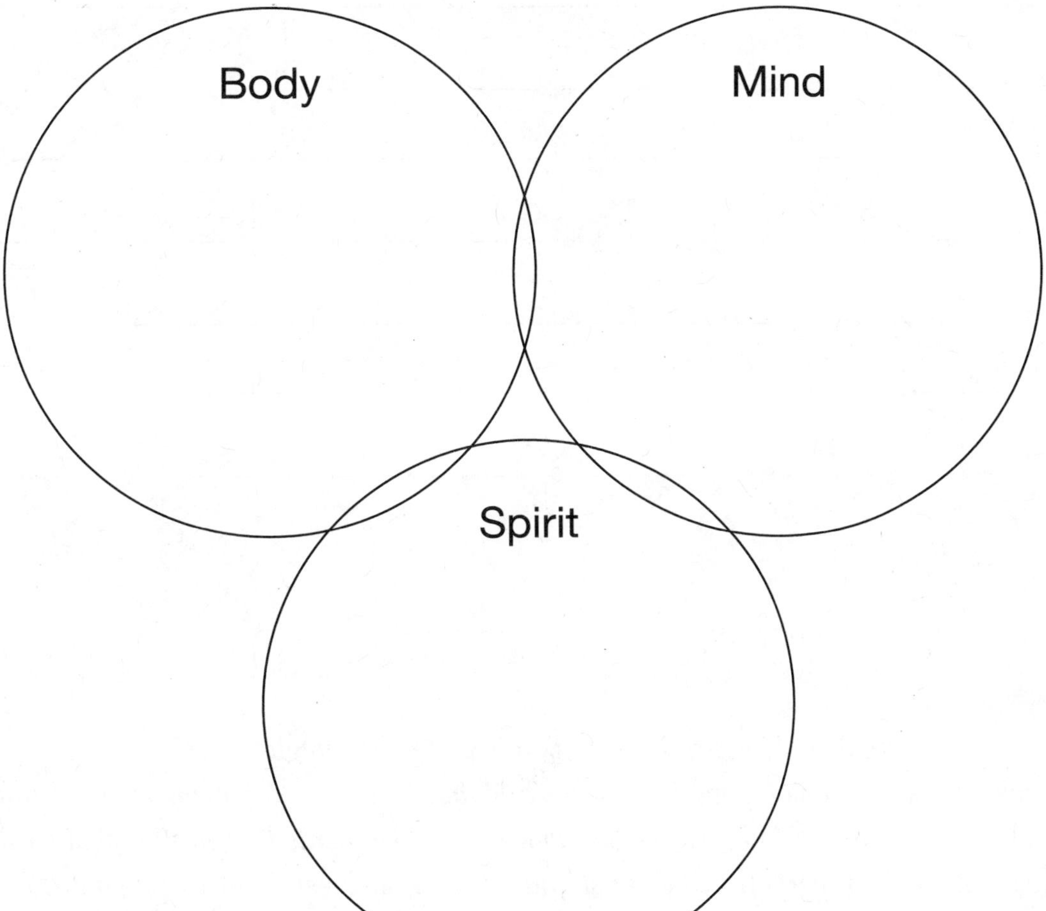

## more to do

You have identified things that you need to do to feel better. How can you incorporate these things into your everyday life? Identify ways to take care of yourself by filling in the spaces below.

Today, I will take care of myself by doing the following things for my

- mind: ______________________________

  ______________________________

  ______________________________

- body: ______________________________

  ______________________________

  ______________________________

- spirit: ______________________________

  ______________________________

  ______________________________

## words of inspiration

*It can be hard to take care of yourself when you have been through something that completely changes how you experience the world, but you have to remember to celebrate your successes. From this day forward, let your accomplishments be a protest against the injustice that has been perpetrated against you. You are successful and triumphant. Let living your life be your revenge.* ~Emily

# learning to breathe 8

## you need to know

Sometimes one of the most important things you can do during moments of intense anxiety or stress is take a deep breath. Deep breathing can help you calm down, let go of stress, and focus on the present moment.

## my story

*After I was raped, the first thing I wanted to do was take a long, hot bath. I needed to feel clean. As I sat in the tub, trying to put together the pieces of what happened, I started to breathe. I made a conscious effort to take deep, slow, cleansing breaths. Taking long, healing breaths calmed my racing thoughts. Breathing helped me find peacefulness and relaxation after being raped. Each breath helped me find an unexpected sense of acceptance and empowerment. I made a choice that while I couldn't change what happened, it wasn't going to ruin my life. By taking one breath at a time, I believed I would get through it.* ~Jessica

When you become distressed, your breathing becomes quick and shallow. This type of shallow breathing is called chest breathing because the short breaths don't reach your abdomen. Shallow breathing increases your heart rate and your blood pressure, and you may do it automatically when you are stressed or angry. One way to calm your mind and body is through abdominal breathing. This type of breathing allows oxygen to flow throughout the body and reduces your heart rate and decreases your blood pressure. When your body is relaxed, your muscles relax, and you are able to better concentrate so you can work through the distressing situation.

# directions

Practice your breathing techniques. Find a quiet distraction-free space with room to sit or lie in a comfortable position.

## *Chest Breathing*

Lie down, place your hand on your chest, and take slow, shallow breaths. Feel your chest rise and fall. Breathe for three counts.

Describe how your body feels after chest breathing.

______________________________________________

______________________________________________

______________________________________________

## *Abdominal Breathing*

Pretend that you have a balloon in your stomach. Place your hand on your abdomen. Take a breath, filling the balloon fully. Slowly exhale and visualize the balloon deflating. Repeat for three counts.

Describe how your body feels after abdominal breathing.

______________________________________________

______________________________________________

______________________________________________

Compare and contrast how your body felt after abdominal breathing versus chest breathing.

## more to do

Over the next few days, pay attention to your breathing. Set an alarm twice a day to practice abdominal breathing. Each day find two convenient five-minute intervals to do nothing but breathe.

I will practice deep breathing the following times each day:

______________________________________________________________________

Some survivors find that they have a difficult time letting their guard down to practice breathing. Understand these are normal feelings, and you can ease in to deep breathing at a slow pace. For example, if you are worried about closing your eyes, start by practicing with your eyes open. If you have a person who makes you feel safe, ask her if she would stay in the room with you during your first few practice sessions. You can tailor this practice to meet your individual needs.

## words of inspiration

*If you have never been taught how to take deep, cleansing breaths by a therapist, it would benefit you greatly to learn how to do this. It calms anxiety and helps ease your pain in certain situations.* ~Jessica

# sleep 9

## you need to know

Nothing can recharge your battery more than a good night's sleep. Sleep is essential for learning, enhancing memory, and maintaining healthy metabolism. There is no way around it: sleep is vital to your emotional and physical well-being.

## my story

*Sleep was important in helping me heal. I had to tell myself that it was okay to take care of myself. I gave myself permission to be tired. Working through my past was physically draining, and I had the right to be exhausted. I let myself rest and recuperate. My body, mind, and soul were healing, and that takes time and rest.* ~Cindy

Unfortunately, for sexual trauma survivors, sleep is often a problem. This may be because you feel stressed or depressed, or it might be because you are suffering from nightmares. (We will address nightmares in detail later in the book. For now, we will focus on general strategies to improve your sleep.) If you are struggling with getting a good night's sleep, establishing a bedtime routine can help. A bedtime routine is a sequence of things that you can do before bed to help yourself settle down to rest. Following a similar routine every night is important in developing good sleep habits.

Here is a list of bedtime dos and don'ts.

## Don't

- Use electronics or watch television an hour before bed.
- Drink sugary or caffeinated beverages three hours before bed.
- Exercise two hours before bed.
- Eat a meal or heavy snack before bed.

## Do

- Enjoy a warm bath before bed (but not too hot or else it'll increase your body temperature, making it difficult to fall asleep).
- Soothe yourself with relaxing music.
- Sip a cup of decaffeinated herbal tea.
- Go to bed each night around the same time.

# directions

Assess your bedtime habits by taking the quiz below.

1. How many hours of sleep do you get each night?

    a. Less than 7

    b. Between 8 to 10

    c. More than 10

2. Do you go to bed at about the same time every night?

    ☐ Yes

    ☐ No

3. Do you drink caffeinated drinks within two hours of going to bed?

    ☐ Yes

    ☐ No

4. Do you snack late at night?

    ☐ Yes

    ☐ No

5. Do you exercise within two hours of going to bed?

    ☐ Yes

    ☐ No

6. Do you check e-mail, visit social media sites, play games, or text before bed?

    ☐ Yes

    ☐ No

7. Do you feel you get enough rest?

   ☐ Yes

   ☐ No

8. Do you nap frequently or have a hard time staying awake during the day?

   ☐ Yes

   ☐ No

9. Do you wake up the same time each morning?

   ☐ Yes

   ☐ No

10. What best describes the place where you sleep?

    a. A place where I can disappear and relax

    b. A workplace where I study

    c. An entertainment room where I watch TV, play games, and search the Internet

11. How would you describe your bedtime routine?

    a. Nonexistent

    b. Hit or miss

    c. Steady or consistent

Here is the answer key for optimal healthy sleep habits.

Yes: Q2, Q7, Q9

No: Q3, Q4, Q5, Q6, Q8

a: Q10

b: Q1

c: Q11

Look over your responses and list some of the problematic areas that stand out and need your immediate attention.

_______________________________________________________________

_______________________________________________________________

_______________________________________________________________

# more to do

A great way to establish a healthy sleep routine is to create a sleep diary. A sleep diary allows you to record information from your bedtime routine that will help you pinpoint sleep problems. Find an online sleep diary template, or set up your own sleep diary using the sample below and the template that follows. For the next week, track your sleep routine and look for patterns that need to be improved.

## sample entry

Date: May 1

Bedtime routine: *(List what you did in the two hours before bed and what you did to settle down before bed.)*

I took a warm shower while listening to music. I organized my stuff for the next day, and I texted a few friends. I snuck a couple of scoops of chocolate ice cream for a sweet treat.

Bedtime: 10 p.m.

Waking time: 5:30 a.m.

Number of times you woke up at night: Once to get a drink of water

Total hours slept: 7.5

Sleep rating: *(On a scale from 1 to 5, rate how well you slept: 1 = not well at all, and 5 = great. Circle your response.)*

1 2 (3) 4 5

Describe how you felt throughout the day.

*I felt a little tired. It took me a while to settle down before I went to sleep. I was still thinking about something a friend texted me, and I woke up thirsty in the middle of the night.*

What changes can you make to improve your bedtime routine for tonight?

*Don't text half an hour before bed. Don't eat a lot of sugar before bed. Need to get to bed earlier so I get at least eight hours of sleep per night.*

What things did you like that you did before bed?

*I loved listening to music while in the shower and getting organized for the next day.*

# your sleep diary

Date: ______________________________

Bedtime routine: *(List what you did in the two hours before bed and what you did to settle down.)*

1. __________________________________ 2. __________________________________

3. __________________________________ 4. __________________________________

5. __________________________________ 6. __________________________________

Bedtime: ___________________________

Waking time: ____________________________

Number of times you woke up at night: ____________

Total hours slept: ______________

Sleep rating: *(On a scale of 1 to 5, rate how well you slept: 1= not well at all. 5 = great. Circle your response.)*

1 2 3 4 5

Describe how you felt throughout the day.

_______________________________________________________________________________

_______________________________________________________________________________

_______________________________________________________________________________

_______________________________________________________________________________

What changes can you make to improve your bedtime routine for tonight?

________________________________________

________________________________________

________________________________________

________________________________________

What things did you like that you did before bed?

________________________________________

________________________________________

________________________________________

________________________________________

## words of inspiration

*Give yourself permission to rest and recuperate. You are doing the very best you can at this time, and when you can do better, you will. Take small steps and just know you are going to do better.* ~Cindy

# 10 exercise

## you need to know

Your physical health is just as important as your emotional health. Because sexual assault is a violation of the body, it's not uncommon for survivors to "zone out" or neglect their physical being. Don't ignore the importance of taking care of your body. Start by being patient with yourself and gradually build exercise into your life. Not only will exercise improve your physical health, but it will also boost your emotional health.

## my story

*I take care of my body by competing in obstacle course races. Racing is my time to show that if I can get through the obstacles on the course, then I can get through the obstacles in my life, including being raped. Obstacle course racing pushes me to my limits both physically and mentally. When I am ready to give up and I feel that I've got nothing left, I push through to the finish line and ring the bell. It's then that I feel like nothing and no one can get me down, as if I'm on top of the world. I believe that I can do and overcome anything life throws at me.* ~Regan

Research shows that just thirty minutes of exercise per day can release the "feel good" chemicals (known as *endorphins*) in your brain that help regulate the emotions that are responsible for self-esteem. The good news is you don't have to be an athlete to exercise regularly; you just need to find an activity that you enjoy doing, and do it. Even small amounts of activity with mild to moderate intensity can make a difference in your mood if you keep it up over time. In fact, regular exercise can produce long-lasting health benefits.

Things to consider when choosing an activity:

1. Find something you enjoy doing. Make it fun so that you'll look forward to it and stick with it. Try a new and exciting exercise such as CrossFit, hula-hooping, kickboxing, Pilates, or skateboarding.

2. Choose something that fits your schedule. For example, if you can't go skiing three times a week, choose something you can do, such as running, walking, or yoga.

3. Choose an indoor and outdoor activity. Have a plan A and a plan B in the event the weather doesn't cooperate with your original plan. Below are some examples.

| **Indoor Activities** | **Outdoor Activities** |
|---|---|
| Aerobics | Cycling |
| Dancing | Golf |
| Weight Training | Running |
| Yoga | Tennis |

4. Plan your exercise routine in advance. Do a week-at-a-glance plan every Sunday and schedule exercise into your week when you can fit it in. Also, be realistic with your goals. For example, if you aren't a morning person, don't force yourself to get up and exercise; odds are you won't stick with it. Also, remember not to exercise too close to your bedtime as it may interfere with your sleep.

# directions

Design your exercise plan.

1. What activities do you enjoy?

______________________________

______________________________

______________________________

2. Choose three indoor and three outdoor activities.

| Indoor | Outdoor |
|---|---|
| 1. | 1. |
| 2. | 2. |
| 3. | 3. |

3. What days and times work best with your schedule? Block off at least thirty minutes three days per week to exercise.

Days: ______________________________

Times: ______________________________

# more to do

If you write down your goals and track them in a fitness chart, you are more likely to make them a reality. Use the chart below to plot your progress.

| Day | Activity | Duration | Feeling Before<br>On a scale of 1 to 5, with 1 being miserable and 5 being great, rate how you felt before and after the activity. | Feeling After |
|---|---|---|---|---|
| Sunday | | | | |
| Monday | | | | |
| Tuesday | | | | |
| Wednesday | | | | |
| Thursday | | | | |
| Friday | | | | |
| Saturday | | | | |

# words of inspiration

*You've got to get back out there and do things for yourself to build yourself back up, and exercise is a great place to start.* ~Regan

# 11 nutrition and well-being

## you need to know

Experiencing sexual trauma can affect your appetite and nutritional habits. It can even lead to eating too much or not enough. This kind of coping, while understandable, can have extreme consequences on your psychological and physical health. Having good dietary habits and giving your body the nutrients it needs to survive will help in your recovery.

## my story

*There was a time when I didn't take care of myself. I didn't eat much, and my appetite became so suppressed that I struggled with eating. I came to a point where I realized I had to stop living this way and take care of myself. I needed to focus on my health. I had to take small steps and force myself to eat something, big or small. Over time and with therapy, I learned to take better care of my body and to nurture my well-being.* ~Cindy

It isn't uncommon for sexual assault survivors to have a complex relationship with food and their body. Food is the fuel your body needs to operate. Just like a car needs gasoline, your body needs nutritious food. Think about it: if you put bad gas into a car, it doesn't run properly and may eventually break down. Similarly, if you fill up on junk food or don't eat enough, then your body cannot perform at its best.

Sexual assault survivors sometimes find unhealthy eating behaviors (overeating or undereating) to be soothing in the short term. After all, it's a way of controlling your body when you might otherwise feel out of control. However, in the long term, this strategy doesn't work. When you don't practice proper nutrition, you will eventually run yourself down. Your body needs nutrients to optimally function.

Below is a chart with some general nutritional recommendations for young women. How close are you to meeting the daily recommendations?

| Teen Girl Daily Nutritional Recommendations |
|---|
| **Fruit and vegetables:** 5 to 7 servings<br><br>**Serving size examples:** 1 cup of leafy vegetables (such as spinach) or 1/2 cup of other vegetables; for a fruit serving, 1 medium-size fruit |
| **Grains (bread, cereal, rice, and pasta):** 6 to 9 servings<br><br>**Serving size examples:** 1 slice of bread, 1 ounce of cereal, or 1/2 cup of pasta |
| **Dairy (milk, yogurt, and cheese):** 2 to 3 servings<br><br>**Serving size examples:** 1 cup of low-fat milk or 1 cup of yogurt |
| **Protein (meat, poultry, fish, dry beans, eggs, and nuts)**: 2 to 3 servings<br><br>**Serving size examples:** 2 to 3 ounces of lean meat, poultry, or fish; 1/2 cup of cooked beans; or 2 tablespoons of peanut butter or almond butter |
| **Water:** drink at least eight 8-ounce glasses daily |

Dietary Guidelines. U.S. Department of Health and Human Services, Office of Disease Prevention and Health Promotion. Available from http://health.gov/dietaryguidelines.

# directions

For today only, pay attention to what you eat. Record your food intake in the table on the next page. At the end of the day, record any thoughts and emotions that stood out before and after you ate something. An example has been provided for you.

Once you've done this, answer the questions that follow.

1. What areas of nutrition do you need to work on? For example, do you need to eat more vegetables or more protein?

______________________________________________

______________________________________________

______________________________________________

2. What thoughts and emotions were you eating in response to?

______________________________________________

______________________________________________

______________________________________________

3. Did you skip meals? If so, what was your reason for missing a meal?

______________________________________________

______________________________________________

______________________________________________

| Day | Breakfast | Lunch | Dinner | Snacks | Thoughts and Emotions Before Meal or Snack | Thoughts and Emotions After Meal or Snack | Things I Can Do Differently |
|---|---|---|---|---|---|---|---|
| Sunday | Skipped | Apple, Peanut Butter Sandwich | Fries and Burger | Chips, Cookie, and Ice Cream | Too many snacks. I was feeling upset, so I kept snacking. | I felt so guilty. This isn't the first time I ate a lot when I was feeling down and out. | Next time I feel this way, I will go for a walk or call a friend until the urge passes. |
| | | | | | | | |

# more to do

For the next week, keep a nutrition log like the one you've just completed. Record what you ate for each meal and any snacks you consumed. Focus on eating a well-balanced diet and pay close attention to your thoughts and emotions. Look for patterns in how your thoughts and emotions may be influencing your eating patterns.

After one week, answer the following questions.

1. What patterns did you notice in your dietary habits?

 ______________________________________________

 ______________________________________________

2. What types of foods did you eat the most?

 ______________________________________________

 ______________________________________________

3. What relationships did you observe between your thoughts and emotions and your eating patterns?

 ______________________________________________

 ______________________________________________

 ______________________________________________

4. In what ways can you improve your dietary habits?

 ______________________________________________

 ______________________________________________

 ______________________________________________

| Day | Breakfast | Lunch | Dinner | Snacks | Thoughts and Emotions Before Meal or Snack | Thoughts and Emotions After Meal or Snack | Things I Can Do Differently |
|---|---|---|---|---|---|---|---|
| Monday | | | | | | | |
| Tuesday | | | | | | | |
| Wednesday | | | | | | | |
| Thursday | | | | | | | |
| Friday | | | | | | | |
| Saturday | | | | | | | |
| Sunday | | | | | | | |

# words of inspiration

*Give yourself permission to take care of your body and nurture your well-being. Your body, mind, and soul are in the process of healing, and they need to recuperate through eating the right foods and getting plenty of rest.* ~Cindy

# emotional well-being 12

## you need to know

Sexual trauma can adversely affect how you feel about yourself. Taking care of your emotional well-being is extremely important. Emotional well-being involves understanding how emotions affect your life and how you can use healthy coping skills to help you reach your full potential.

## my story

*I knew that getting into therapy was going to be the best thing for me, but that was only a few hours a week for a period of time after my attack. I was scared and didn't know how I would manage to cope with my time and thoughts the rest of the time. I had to find a way to make sure that I didn't go crazy. Although many people knew about the rape, time passed, and I had days when I felt down and upset. Sometimes I still have those days. I found that along with therapy, I could help myself feel better by focusing on my emotional well-being. I would use social media sites, books, and the Internet to find quotes, spiritual verses, and other sayings to inspire me. This has been a huge help for me to express and connect with how I am feeling.* ~Gabby

Just as you can take care of your physical well-being, you can also care for your emotional well-being. Below are some strategies to help you get started.

1. Do something nice for yourself.

   Think of things that make you feel good, such as going for a stroll outdoors, basking in the sunshine, pampering yourself with a manicure, or sipping cocoa while listening to your favorite song.

2. Don't hang on to unhealthy or unproductive thoughts.

   Thoughts aren't 100 percent true. Don't put too much time and energy into untrue self-depleting thoughts. Many survivors have hurtful thoughts like, *I'll never be good enough,* or *Nobody loves me.* There are two keys to overcoming this way of thinking. First, think of how you would respond if a good friend said that about herself. Wouldn't you tell her that there was a different way to look at that self-defeating thought? Second, let difficult thoughts pass by without becoming too bothered by their actual content. Remember, these thoughts are just a few of hundreds that you have every day, so you don't need to overvalue any specific thought.

3. Focus on the present.

   Today is all that you have. Focusing on the past won't change anything, and worrying about the future won't change the past. While it is natural to want to understand what happened to you and why it happened, you can learn techniques that will bring you back to the present. You can focus on deep breathing, go for a walk, wash the dishes and feel the warm water on your hands, or feel your feet on the floor beneath you. In short, learn to focus on the sights and sounds of the present moment.

4. Don't bully yourself.

   Don't stand for self-bullying. If you were to see someone bullying another person, wouldn't you intervene? Why would you let yourself be bullied without doing something about it? Don't call yourself names and put yourself down. If you are placing too much value on a painful thought, decide whether it is 100 percent true. Chances are it is not.

5. Focus on your strengths.

   Everyone has strengths, things they are good at. Sometimes we put the spotlight on our weakness and forget to give ourselves credit for our accomplishments. Be sure to acknowledge and celebrate your successes.

# directions

Using the five steps to improving emotional well-being, identify areas you want to work on to improve your emotional well-being. In each footprint, respond to the prompt given to discover what you need to do to achieve emotional wellness.

1. List things you enjoy doing.

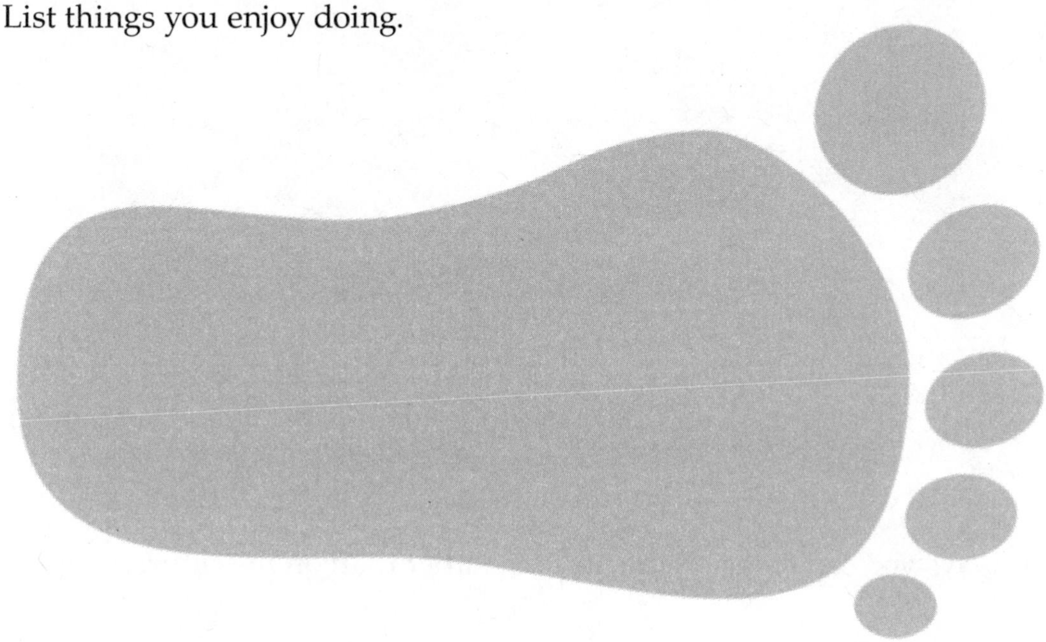

2. List the hurtful thought(s) that you need to look at in a different way.

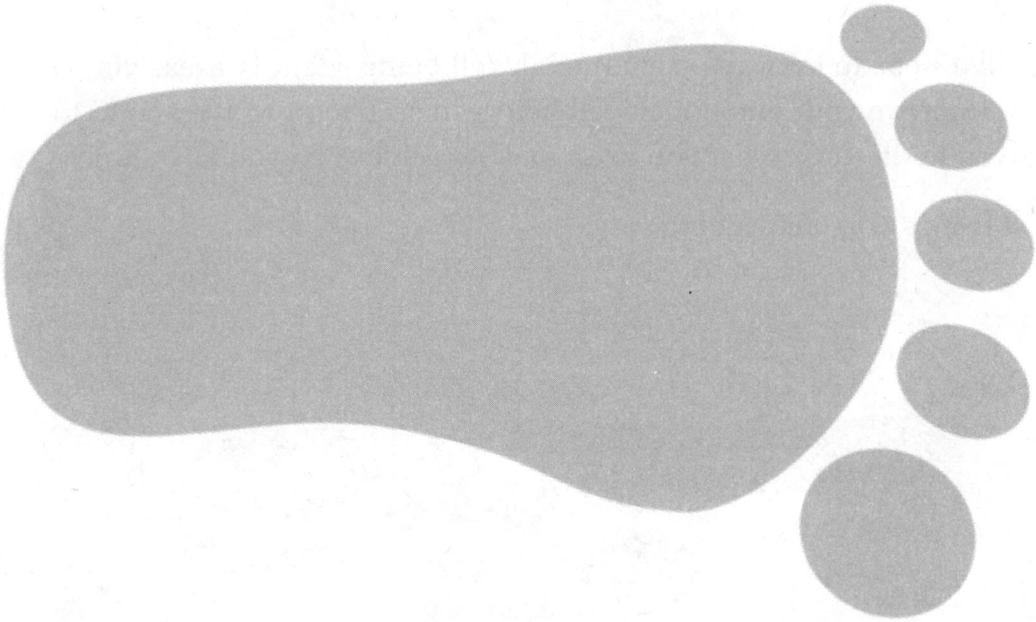

3. List ways you can focus on the present, rather than on the future or the past.

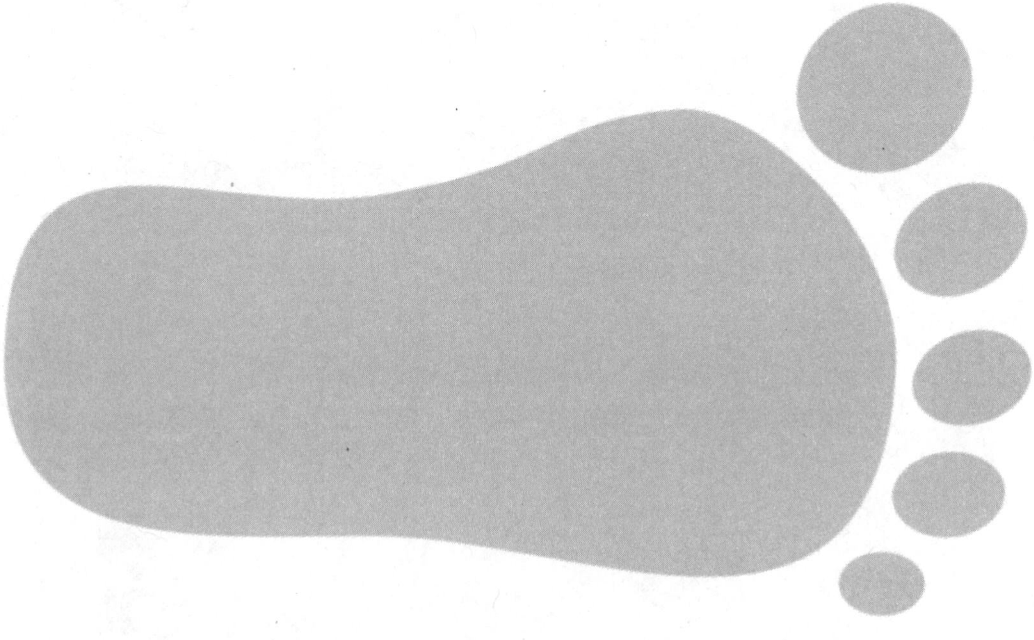

4. List ways that you bully yourself and ways you can be kinder to yourself.

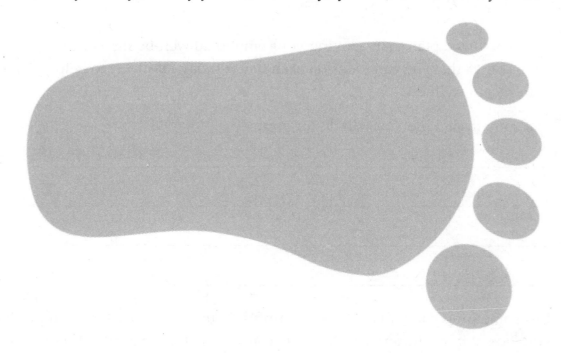

5. List at least three strengths or accomplishments.

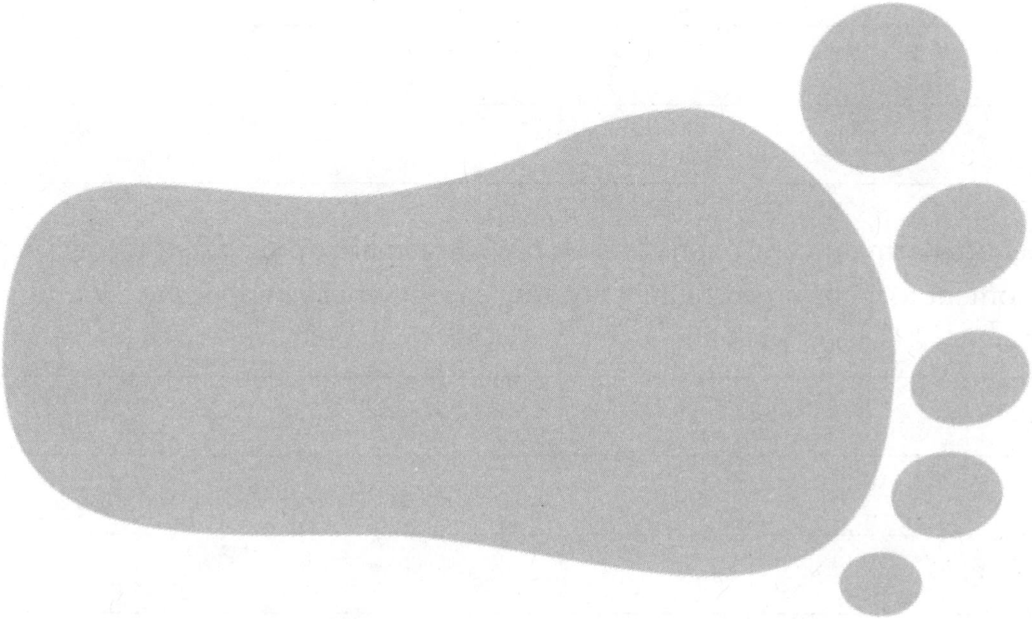

# more to do

Create a personalized plan to improving your emotional well-being. For each prompt, write down things that you can focus on each day ("Today I will…") to help you achieve emotional wellness.

1. List something kind you will do for yourself.

 ______________________________

 ______________________________

 ______________________________

 ______________________________

2. List something you will do when a painful thought surfaces. For example, will you look at it in a different way or tell yourself that these kinds of thoughts are common and you don't have to let them overwhelm you?

 ______________________________

 ______________________________

 ______________________________

 ______________________________

3. Set an alarm on your phone and stop what you are doing when it rings. Take that moment to focus on absolutely nothing except what's happening around you.

 ______________________________

 ______________________________

 ______________________________

 ______________________________

4. When you bully yourself, what will you do? Think of what you would say if you saw someone bullying another person. Have this same conversation with yourself if you find you are engaging in self-bullying.

____________________________________________

____________________________________________

____________________________________________

____________________________________________

5. List an activity, exercise, project, hobby, or something else that you excel in.

____________________________________________

____________________________________________

____________________________________________

____________________________________________

## words of inspiration

*There are so many ways for you to express and nurture your emotional well-being. Taking care of yourself helps you realize that you are on a path that has a purpose.* ~Gabby

# 13 acceptance

## you need to know

Thoughts and feelings come and go like the waves of the ocean. Although they can seem completely overwhelming, they will naturally pass on their own if you learn to accept them for what they are. Allowing your thoughts and feelings to freely come and go is known as acceptance.

## my story

*Rape was a defining moment in my life, but I knew that I couldn't let it define who I am. Rather, I had to define it. I had to learn to be okay with my feelings and emotions and not let them hold me back. I had to learn that it's harder when I fight them. So I made a choice to let them freely come and go and not fight them.* ~Joi

Acceptance isn't the same as being okay with being victimized. Rather, it refers to accepting your thoughts and emotions and riding them out when they happen, like waves in an ocean.

Have you ever watched a wave on the beach crash on the shoreline, weaken, and drift back into the ocean? Its intensity and force is strong when it hits the sand, but it doesn't seem so powerful when it drifts back to sea. Feelings and waves have a lot in common. Just like waves, some feelings are powerful, and some are weak. Regardless of their intensity, one thing remains true—the waves of thought find their way back to the sea.

Metaphors, such as the waves of emotion, can help you understand how acceptance works. Accepting your thoughts and emotions means allowing them to exist and letting them pass naturally. Use the tips below to help you gain awareness and ride the wave of difficult thoughts and emotions.

## Acceptance Tips

1. Acknowledge your thoughts and feelings and try to name them. For example, if you're overwhelmed by anxiety, tell yourself, *I am feeling anxious.* Don't avoid or fight your feelings. You'll only prolong their presence and make them stronger. Acknowledge them, name them, and allow them to roll back into the sea.

2. Keep in mind that thoughts and feelings can't hurt or harm you. Just as waves wash ashore at different intensities, so can thoughts and feelings. If the impact of a thought or feeling feels overwhelming, tell yourself, *I can roll with the tide and ride this one out while keeping my feet planted firmly in the sand.*

3. Celebrate getting through rough waves. When you choose to ride the wave and not fight it, you will feel more empowered and in the process grow into a stronger and more resilient person.

# directions

Riding out difficult waves and learning the art of acceptance is not an easy task. In fact, it takes time and patience. Explore ways you can use acceptance in your life by responding to the prompts below.

Describe a time when you experienced a difficult emotional wave.

______________________________________________________________

______________________________________________________________

______________________________________________________________

______________________________________________________________

______________________________________________________________

______________________________________________________________

Using the acceptance tips, respond to the prompts below to guide yourself through your past experience.

1. Name any difficult or painful emotions and thoughts you recall experiencing. Name the emotions: Were you depressed, embarrassed, or stressed?

   I was feeling: ______________________________________________

   ______________________________________________________________

   ______________________________________________________________

Recognize the thoughts: What unhelpful thoughts did you experience?

I was thinking: ________________________________________

________________________________________

________________________________________

2. Imagine revisiting that experience and seeing it from a different perspective. Rather than fighting the wave, practice accepting it and riding it out. As you imagine yourself riding the wave, describe how you felt afterward.

________________________________________

________________________________________

________________________________________

3. Celebrate making it through rough times. When you ride a wave, you come out feeling more centered. Take time to acknowledge and celebrate your accomplishments. List something good you will do for yourself the next time you get through an intense wave.

________________________________________

________________________________________

________________________________________

# more to do

Using metaphors, such as ocean waves, to describe thoughts and feelings is a great way to help you make sense of difficult times. Another great coping tool is a visual reminder. Make your own wave bottle, and let it serve as a visual reminder to allow your feelings to come and go like waves in an ocean.

Here is what you'll need:

1. Clear bottle with a cap (a water bottle works great)
2. Blue or green food coloring
3. Oil (mineral oil and baby oil both work)

## directions

Fill your bottle two-thirds full of oil. Fill the remainder of the bottle with water. Add a few drops of food coloring. Securely cap the bottle (to prevent leakage, tape on the lid). Place the bottle on its side, and rock it back and forth, from side to side. Watch as the waves form and then settle again. Use this bottle as a visual reminder that in your life waves will form and eventually settle again. No matter how intense the wave, it will subside just like the wave you create in the bottle. Stop fighting your thoughts and emotions and allow them to come and go naturally… Practice acceptance.

# words of inspiration

*Don't fight your feelings. Your healing journey is an individual one. At the end of the day, you have to take care of yourself and do what's best for you.* ~Joi

# self-soothing behaviors 14

## you need to know

Self-soothing behaviors are the simple, nurturing, and kind things that you do to make yourself feel better. They help calm, ease, and settle your discomfort, and they can make hard times more manageable. When life throws you a curve ball, one of the best things you can do is learn to soothe yourself.

## my story

*I soothe myself by being in tune with my environment. I take care and put effort in to creating an atmosphere that is comfortable and engages all of my senses. For example, I make sure that my room is clean and nicely decorated. I play soft yoga music, light a candle, and sip tea. Paying attention to my surroundings gives me the space to cope with stressful situations. In this relaxing atmosphere, I find my senses calm down, and I am able to process my thoughts and feelings. Keeping a soothing environment helps me live a focused life.* ~Camryn

Often people don't take time to notice the little things they can do to make themselves feel better. Whether it's smelling homemade cookies baking in the oven or snuggling with a favorite blanket, there are small things that surround us that make a difference. It's these small things that help soothe and comfort us in our times of need. Our senses play a big role in helping to comfort us.

When creating a self-soothing experience, it's important to tap into each sense to find pleasure. These may be things that you enjoy but often take for granted, such as the feel of sand between your toes or studying the vivid colors of a rainbow after it rains. No matter how small these things seem, they play an instrumental part in your recovery. Below are some examples of things that may be soothing.

### Hearing

- the sound of birds chirping
- the echo of waves crashing onto the shore
- the melody of your favorite song

### Seeing

- the display of twinkling stars in the night sky
- the vision of rain drops trickling down a pane of glass
- the photograph capturing a fond memory

### Smelling

- the scent of homemade cookies
- the smell of fresh-cut grass
- the fragrance of your favorite candle

### Tasting

- the cold sweetness of ice cream
- the taste of a soothing, warm, sweet beverage
- the saltiness of buttery popcorn

### Touching

- the feel of smooth velvet
- the lushness of faux fur
- the texture of sand escaping through your fingers

# directions

Treat yourself to a self-soothing experience by tapping into each of your senses. Identify things that soothe you during difficult times. After identifying some things you enjoy, take time to indulge in a soothing experience.

## Hearing

What are some sounds that you enjoy hearing?

______________________________________________

______________________________________________

______________________________________________

## Seeing

What are some things that you enjoy looking at?

______________________________________________

______________________________________________

______________________________________________

## Smelling

What are some scents that you enjoy smelling?

______________________________________________

______________________________________________

______________________________________________

## Tasting

What flavors do you enjoy tasting?

______________________________________________

______________________________________________

______________________________________________

## Touching

What textures do you enjoy feeling?

______________________________________________

______________________________________________

______________________________________________

## more to do

Make a self-soothing kit. Choose five soothing sensory items and place them in a special box (a decorated shoe box works great) or a cosmetic bag. If one of your items is perishable, be sure to replace it after you use it and pay attention to the expiration date. Here are some examples of items you may want to consider.

**Hearing:** wind chime

**Seeing:** photograph

**Smelling:** lavender oil

**Tasting:** stick of gum

**Touching:** piece of silk

Place your self-soothing kit in a convenient place and make it your "go-to" box when you need some soothing comfort.

## words of inspiration

*Take care and put value into creating an atmosphere that is comfortable and engages all of your senses. Allow your whole self to be present in the moment. After sexual trauma, you may feel devalued. No one else is going to give you your value back. Be willing to give yourself that gift in a way that encourages your healing process.* ~Camryn

# 15 healing through writing

## you need to know

It has been said that writing is a window to the soul. Writing is a creative form of expression that allows you to explore your innermost thoughts. Writing has been shown to help survivors of trauma heal by helping them come to terms with what has happened and let go of guilt and self-blame.

## my story

*Journaling helped me cope with the rape. What has been empowering at the low points in my life has been going back and rereading my journal. Seeing what I wrote in the past helps me see how far I have come in my life. The thing I like about writing is I can write whatever I want. If I want to tell my assailant off, I can. If I want to curse, I can. Writing is freedom to express your innermost thoughts and feelings. Just be sure to keep it in a safe and secure location.* ~Joi

Now you may be thinking, *The last thing that I want to do is write about how I feel*, but if you give it a chance, you may find writing to be a wonderful therapeutic tool to help you sort through and clarify your thoughts and feelings. Writing can help you discover patterns, and with time, you can try to change some of the thoughts that might be causing you the most distress. For example, you may find that when you write, you are constantly struggling with whether or not you are a good person or whether or not you are loveable. Through writing, you can explore healthier ways to deal with your thoughts and notice any habitual problematic thinking patterns that surface. For example, instead of, "I think I failed miserably," you can write it in a more balanced way, "I didn't get the outcome I wanted, but I give myself credit for trying."

# directions

Journaling can help you look back on different times in your life and see how you got through them. It's a great tool for identifying your strengths and areas where you are coping well, and for exploring areas you want to improve on.

Put these journaling tips into your everyday life and use writing as a tool to help you cope.

## *Four Tips for Journaling*

1. **Keep your journal with you at all times. Don't leave home without it.**

   Ideas, thoughts, and emotions are free-flowing. Capture the moment by writing about it when it occurs, otherwise you may forget to include it in your journal.

2. **Make your journal special.**

   Whether it's a book or a spiral notebook, choose a journal that specially designed for you. It's not about how it looks, but how often you use it.

3. **Make it a habit.**

   Decide how often you want to write (maybe every day, or a few days a week), and set aside at least fifteen minutes to journal.

4. **Don't worry about grammar, spelling, or any other rules.**

   Unlike schoolwork, journaling is free from rules. You can write about anything you want, and grammar, punctuation, and syntax don't matter. Your entry can be as long or as short as you want it to be.

Write about anything that comes to mind. Here are some examples of things that you can include in your journal:

- things you are excited about
- reactions to situations
- emotions that you are experiencing
- inspirational quotes that you came across
- things that are bugging you

## more to do

As you write, look for patterns in your thoughts, feelings, and behaviors. For example:

- Are you constantly blaming yourself for things?
- Do you feel unworthy of respect?
- Do your emotions fluctuate?
- Are most of your journal entries unhappy or worried?

Pay attention to negative patterns in your writing, situations that cause uneasiness, and the dialogue that you have with yourself. By acknowledging unhelpful patterns, you will learn better ways to work through your troubling experiences.

## words of inspiration

*When I go back and read my past journal entries, I say to myself,* I may not be where I want to be right now, but I sure have come a long way on my journey. *Healing is a process that occurs at your own pace. Use journaling as a tool to help you heal.* ~Joi

# 16 progressive muscle relaxation

## you need to know

The body responds to stressful thoughts and situations with muscle tension, which can cause physical pain and discomfort. One way to relax your muscles and reduce stress is by practicing *progressive muscle relaxation* (PMR). PMR is a proven technique that involves tensing specific muscles and then relaxing them while creating physical awareness and mentally letting go of stress.

## my story

*I learned how to relax my muscles, unwind, and slow down when I got into yoga. Aside from counseling, yoga was the most therapeutic and relaxing thing I did for myself. It helped me relax and better focus. My mood improved, and as a result, I found myself smiling a lot more. Learning to relax and unwind had a positive effect on my mind-set, which in turn helped me heal.* ~Eliza

PMR has been used for years in the treatment of anxiety, insomnia, depression, and stress. Here are just some of the benefits of PMR:

- alleviates stress and anxiety
- promotes deep and relaxing abdominal breathing
- energizes and increases stamina
- improves your ability to focus
- improves sleep

Now you can apply this helpful technique in your own life.

# directions

PMR only involves two steps:

1. Tensing your muscles
2. Releasing your muscles while mentally letting go of stress

Give it a try!

First, describe how your body feels before the exercise.

________________________________________________________________

________________________________________________________________

________________________________________________________________

________________________________________________________________

Next, find a quiet, discreet location and get into a comfortable position. If your mind begins to wander, gently bring it back and focus only on the muscle group you are tensing. If you feel pain when tensing a muscle group, you can skip that muscle group.

Starting with your feet, tighten them by curling your toes. Tense your muscles until you feel mild tension on the targeted muscle group. Now release the muscles back to a relaxed state. Feel the difference between tensing and relaxing your muscles. Next, tighten your calf muscles. Again, slowly release the muscles to a state of relaxation. Now tense your thigh muscles. Let them go and relax, noticing the difference. Tighten your abdomen and chest by taking a deep breath and holding it. Slowly exhale all of the air from your lungs. Next, stiffen your jaw by scrunching up your face and squinting your eyes. Now, let your mouth drop open and your eyes droop. Feel the difference. Make tight fists with your hands. Then let your palms slowly open and your fingers completely relax. If you want to repeat any of the muscle groups, do so until you feel more calm and relaxed.

On the lines below compare and contrast how your body felt when your muscles were in a state of tension compared to when they were in a relaxed state.

______________________________________________

______________________________________________

______________________________________________

______________________________________________

How can you use PMR to help you in stressful situations?

______________________________________________

______________________________________________

______________________________________________

______________________________________________

______________________________________________

# more to do

PMR is a great tool you can use discreetly anytime and anywhere. With practice, you can do it whenever you need to calm down, and no one will ever know.

Note: If you practice PMR every day (for example, before you go to sleep), you will eventually be able to use it during times of high anxiety and stress. Try doing PMR at various times throughout the day. At the end of the day, write where you used PMR and how you felt afterward.

Where: ____________________________________________

____________________________________________

____________________________________________

____________________________________________

How you felt: ____________________________________________

____________________________________________

____________________________________________

____________________________________________

# words of inspiration

*Being able to mindfully relax is a great way to slow down your brain and bring calmness to the outside world. It helps you find peace within yourself and lets you live in the present moment.* ~Eliza

# 17 engaging in mindfulness

## you need to know

After experiencing a traumatic event, it may be difficult to focus on the present. You may feel trapped in the past or in fear of the future. Regardless of whether your mind takes you backward or forward, it's important to train yourself to stay grounded in the here and now. Learning to engage and live in the present moment is called *mindfulness.*

## my story

*My road to recovery has been a journey. When you grow up in a sexually abusive home, you learn to hyperfocus on your abuser's whereabouts and movements, which can lead to fear and anxiety. I had to break that cycle and focus not on what was out there, but rather on what was inward and on listening to myself. I had to be mindful of my thoughts, feelings, and surroundings. Once I was able to do that, I could start the healing process.* ~Theresa

Mindfulness is purposely engaging in, focusing on, and living in the present moment. It is about tapping in to each of your senses and relating to your body, feelings, and thoughts. When you live in the moment, you don't have to fight thoughts of the past or distract yourself from thinking too far into the future. Mindfulness teaches you to slow down and pay purposeful attention to what is happening around you.

# directions

Your senses provide the key to helping you center yourself in the present moment. Below are some activities for you to practice that focus on using your senses to engage in mindfulness. Rather than doing all of the senses at once, spread them out over the course of a couple of days. For today, start with two senses.

For this activity, you will need a timing device, and a pen and paper. For each sense, set your timer for three minutes. If your mind wanders, just remember to breathe and gently bring yourself back to the present activity. After you finish the activity, use the space provided to write down any thoughts, feelings, or emotions you experienced.

## Smell

Find a scent that you enjoy smelling, for example, a fragrant candle, perfume, or coffee beans. For the next three minutes, focus on the item's scent. Does it smell comforting, refreshing, or sweet?

Describe any thoughts, feelings, or emotions:

## Sight

Find something interesting to look at, such as a colorful painting, a beautiful landscape, or a blade of grass. Whatever you choose, make sure it's something that you find appealing. For the next three minutes, study the item's shape(s), color(s), border(s), movement(s), and other features. Pay special attention to every detail. If your mind starts to wander, gently bring your attention back to the item.

Describe any thoughts, feelings, or emotions:

______________________________________________

______________________________________________

______________________________________________

______________________________________________

______________________________________________

## Sound

For the next few minutes, focus on the sounds around you. Or find an instrumental song, a waterfall, the hum of traffic, or some other sound to listen to.

Describe any thoughts, feelings, or emotions:

______________________________________________

______________________________________________

______________________________________________

______________________________________________

______________________________________________

## Taste

Focus on tasting what you're eating. Take a bite of a food item you enjoy. Pay special attention to the taste, texture, sweetness, tartness, and juiciness. Let the flavor fill your mouth and enjoy each bite.

Describe any thoughts, feelings, or emotions:

______________________________________________

______________________________________________

______________________________________________

______________________________________________

______________________________________________

## Touch

Find something that has an interesting texture to touch. Pick up the item. Does it feel soft, cuddly, plush, or smooth? Notice how the item feels against your skin.

Describe any thoughts, feelings, or emotions:

______________________________________________

______________________________________________

______________________________________________

______________________________________________

______________________________________________

## more to do

Make it a priority to take time each day to stop and focus on the moment at hand. For the next five days, choose one of the mindful techniques above to practice. Once you get good at tapping into each sense, you can begin to combine your senses. For example, you can focus on listening to soothing music while cuddling with your favorite throw as the aroma of a lavender candle fills the air. Of course when you start focusing on more than one sense, you'll want to devote more time to the exercise because there will be a lot more to experience.

## words of inspiration

*Allow yourself to be happy, sad, angry, and scared. You don't have to pretend everything is fine when it's not. It's okay to work through your emotions no matter how difficult they are. Become mindful of your thoughts, feelings, and surroundings. Mindfulness helps you become centered on what's happening right now, and that can be very healing.* ~Theresa

# guided imagery 18

## you need to know

After a traumatic experience, it's important to find ways to cope, release, and relax. When you want nothing more than to take a break from your world, you can use guided imagery to help you travel anywhere your heart desires. *Guided imagery* is a technique in which you visualize a peaceful place and mentally immerse yourself in the setting.

## my story

*It's good to have images picked out in your mind beforehand so you can readily call them up when you need to mentally escape. When I get in those moments, I ask myself, Where do I want to be right now? In the past, sometimes I would use guided imagery to get myself out of the abusive situation. I would envision a better life for myself. I remember when I would see an airplane, I would imagine being on it and going to a better place, a better life. I envisioned a better future for myself, and I made sure that I made that dream a reality.* ~Theresa

Do you remember playing as a child and being anyone you wanted to be—maybe a rock star, an actress, a doctor, or a chef? Did you know that you can use the same imagination you used as a child to help you cope as you get older? Guided imagery is a tool that can help you purposefully go to a calmer, more relaxed place. All you need to do is close your eyes and let your mind focus on the places you've always wanted to go.

Your imagination holds the key to helping you relax. It is normal for trauma survivors to sometimes have frightening or unwanted thoughts when they let their mind relax. They may worry that they are becoming too disconnected from what is happening in the present moment. If this happens to you, simply take a deep breath and open your eyes. Remind yourself that you are in a safe place, feeling the air flowing in and out of your nose. When you are ready, you can go back to the imaginary scene of your choice.

# directions

We all need a special place that helps us feel calm and grounded. Imagine taking a mental vacation and getting a much-needed break from your everyday life.

How to engage in guided imagery:

1. Take a minute to focus on how you are feeling right now. Are your thoughts racing? Is your body tense? Do you feel upset?

2. Now, think of a place you would like to go. This could be a place you've visited in the past that holds fond memories, or it could be a peaceful or joyful place you've always wanted to visit. For example, is your place of refuge somewhere you've vacationed, such as a beach, an amusement park, or a mountain getaway? Or is it some place you've always wanted to visit like the Golden Gate Bridge in San Francisco or the Taj Mahal in India?

3. Describe the details of your dream destination.

   Where are you? ______________________________

   ______________________________

   ______________________________

   What do you see around you? ______________________________

   ______________________________

   ______________________________

   What fragrances fill the air? ______________________________

   ______________________________

   ______________________________

What sounds surround you? ____________________

____________________

____________________

4. Get ready to imagine the scene. Set a timer for at least one minute. Place your hand on your abdomen. Take few deep, relaxing breaths. Allow the air to flow all the way into your belly.

5. Close your eyes and imagine yourself in that special place. It's exactly as you dreamed it would be.

6. After one minute, describe how your body and mind are responding to your mental vacation. For example, are you muscles less tense? Are you calmer? Has your breathing deepened?

____________________

____________________

____________________

____________________

____________________

# more to do

Guided imagery is great way to keep your dream destination with you at all times. Make a visual reminder of your dream destination by recreating it on your computer or on paper. Create a screen saver, a paper collage, or a scrapbook of your scene, or you can draw or paint a picture of your imagery. Keep this visual reminder close at hand and retreat to it any time you need to go to a calmer, more peaceful place in your mind.

# words of inspiration

> *Use imagery to envision a different future for yourself, use it to dream, or use it to escape what's happening around you. Guided imagery can help you imagine something better for yourself, and if you can see it, you can work toward it.* ~Theresa

# 19 life scripts

## you need to know

*Life scripts* are the meanings and messages that you attached to events that happened to you. Depending on your script, you may interpret an event in a number of different ways, and your behavior will be in response to your interpretation of what happened. When life scripts are more of a hindrance than a help, it's time to change them into something more positive and supportive.

## my story

*There will always be good and bad days whether it's one day after your incident or one decade. Be patient with yourself and tell yourself positive things. Each day you will grow and find ways to cope with your emotions, and each day you will grow stronger than you ever thought you could be.* ~Gabby

# *Life Scripts*

Everyone has scripts they play repeatedly in their mind. Some scripts are helpful while others are hurtful. People who have experienced trauma often play hurtful scripts to themselves such as:

*I'm not good enough.*

*I can never trust another person.*

*No one will protect me.*

*I'm a bad person.*

*I'm not normal.*

Unfortunately, if these scripts are played repeatedly, they can result in low self-esteem and a poor self-image. You don't have to let your scripts limit your life. You have the power to rewrite them into something more productive and helpful. For example:

*I'm not good enough.* → *I am as worthy as everyone else.*

*I can never trust another person.* → *There are trustworthy people whom I can learn to trust with time.*

*No one will protect me.* → *I can learn how to figure out the people who care about me by the way they treat me over time.*

*I'm a bad person.* → *No one deserves to be victimized. What happened to me was bad, but it doesn't make me a bad person.*

*I'm not normal.* → *It is perfectly normal for me to have reactions to the things I've experienced. I can learn how to cope with these reactions.*

Research has shown that if people work on changing unhelpful thought patterns, they can live a more fulfilling life.

If you struggle with unhelpful life scripts, use the following steps to revise them:

1. Identify the unhelpful scripts and make it a priority to change them.
2. Pay attention to how the unhelpful script affects your thoughts, feelings, and behaviors.
3. Revise and rewrite your unhelpful script into a more positive one like the examples above. To help you do this, you might think of how a supportive friend might respond to your statement. You can also consider whether a statement is always true or if there are other ways to look at the situation. If you feel stuck, consider finding a trusted adult or mental health professional to help you.
4. Practice your new script so that the unhelpful script fades into the background and the new script takes the lead.

# directions

Imagine all of your unhelpful scripts displayed on a computer screen. You are an editor, and your job is to change the unhelpful messages into more helpful ones. In the table below, write down your negative messages and change them to more helpful and supportive ones.

| Unhelpful Script | Helpful Script |
|---|---|
| 1. | |
| 2. | |
| 3. | |
| 4. | |
| 5. | |

## more to do

Make a copy of the new helpful life scripts that you wrote. Tape them to your mirror, place them on your nightstand, or keep them in a convenient location. When you tell yourself something unhelpful, recite the new helpful script out loud over and over until you begin to believe what you wrote.

## words of inspiration

*Build yourself up with positive messages. Your experience can help you grow into a strong person. You will be a force to be reckoned with once you reach deep down and find out how much strength and power you truly have.* ~Gabby

# choosing healthy coping skills 20

## you need to know

Sometimes when people go through difficult times, they use self-destructive coping methods that temporarily alleviate the pain, but are harmful in the long run. For example, drinking alcohol, cutting, taking drugs, and having risky sex may provide temporary relief, but once the rush is gone, the feeling of emptiness still exists. Fortunately, there are countless healthy coping skills that can promote healing, health, and vitality.

## my story

*No matter how hard I tried to forget about the rape, I couldn't. It started manifesting itself in other ways, and it was affecting my life. I started to drink, gained weight, and didn't take care of myself. Sometimes I felt like I was dying inside. I would go through bouts of depression. I would often drink as a means to cope. I wouldn't even have the energy to get dressed or groom myself. I knew I was sad and depressed but didn't know why. Then there came a time that I realized I couldn't go on living this unhealthy lifestyle. I had to take care of myself. I decided I wanted to do something good rather than detrimental. So, I stopped drinking and started taking care of myself. I got involved with helping others who were traumatized by sexual abuse. As a result, today I travel across the United States and speak with others who are on the road to recovery from sexual abuse.* ~Joi

Unhealthy coping skills are destructive ways that people cope with life experiences. For example, smoking might be a way to cope with stress in the short term, but it could lead to cancer. Unprotected sex may temporarily feel good, but it can lead to pregnancy and sexually transmitted infections. These coping skills are detrimental to your long-term healing.

Healthy coping skills can help you deal with stress in ways that don't hurt your mind or body. They can be distracting, enjoyable, or relaxing. Examples of healthy coping skills include talking to trustworthy friends, going for a walk or jog, or learning a new hobby. There are countless healthy coping skills. You just have to find the right fit for you.

# directions

At some point in time, most people have engaged in some form of self-destructive behavior. The question isn't if you engage in these behaviors, but how often and why? Do you engage in healthy or destructive coping skills? Take the quiz below to see.

True or false (circle T or F)?

I frequently…

| | | |
|---|---|---|
| make unhealthy and impulsive decisions. | T | F |
| take unnecessary and dangerous risks. | T | F |
| will do anything, even if it's unhealthy, to feel loved. | T | F |
| feel like I need to prove I am in control. | T | F |
| act wild and crazy, doing things I later regret. | T | F |
| feel confused and don't understand why I do the things that I do. | T | F |
| am afraid of letting people see the "real me." | T | F |

Circle all of the harmful behaviors that you engage in.

I often…

- overeat to comfort myself.
- withhold food to feel in control.
- avoid people because I do not feel deserving of friendship.
- drink alcohol to escape.
- smoke cigarettes to deal with stress.
- take drugs to escape.
- let others mistreat me.
- neglect my personal hygiene.
- feel ashamed to ask for help.
- cut or harm myself.
- engage in unprotected sex.

List any other destructive behaviors you use to cope.

________________________________________

________________________________________

________________________________________

Complete each statement below.

In the short term, my harmful behaviors help me:

Example: *Distract myself from my pain, deal with my anxiety, or punish myself because I feel I'm not worth it*

______________________________________________________________

______________________________________________________________

______________________________________________________________

The following things trigger my destructive behaviors:

Example: *Drinking helps me numb myself when I have memories of the trauma.*

______________________________________________________________

______________________________________________________________

______________________________________________________________

I feel ________________ after I have engaged in ______________________.

Example: *I feel ashamed and guilty when I overeat to make myself feel better.*

______________________________________________________________

______________________________________________________________

______________________________________________________________

I would like to change the following destructive behaviors:

Example: *Compulsively spending money*

___

___

___

Note: If at any time you are putting yourself in harm's way, feel addicted to a substance, or have thoughts of hurting yourself or someone else, please seek professional help immediately. This is not something you should try to conquer on your own.

# more to do

The key to working through situations in which you act out destructively is to plan ahead by identifying a healthy coping skill you can use in place of the unhealthy one. On the list below, mark the healthy coping skills you can substitute in place of destructive ones. Imagine using the healthy skill the next time you are in a situation when you are tempted to do something unhealthy. When you practice healthy coping skills over a period of weeks and months, you will start to see positive benefits both physically and mentally.

### Productive Coping Skills

Cleaning

Doodling or drawing

Exercising (walking, yoga, and so forth)

Painting your nails

Watching a movie

Doing your homework

Playing a game

Talking to a friend

Going to the mall

Singing

Playing an instrument

Taking a bath or shower

Dancing

Baking or cooking

Organizing your room

Pampering yourself with a home spa treatment

Putting together a puzzle

List your own:

______________________________

______________________________

# words of inspiration

*Remember where you are today will not be where you are tomorrow. The road to healing is a process, and you have to take care of yourself to make progress on your journey.* ~Joi

# 21 coping with nightmares

## you need to know

After experiencing sexual trauma, you may find that you're suffering from fitful sleep or frightening nightmares. A lack of sleep can create high levels of anxiety and stress. If you struggle with nightmares, you can learn skills to change them by altering the ending to a neutral or more pleasant one. The process of changing a dream's ending while you are awake is known as *imagery rehearsal*.

## my story

*I had recurrent and frightening nightmares that terrified me for years. As a way of working through my dreams, I would write them down right after I awoke. Writing helped me work through the memories of my father molesting me. It helped me get in touch and connect with my hurt inner child. I realized my dreams were my body's way of saying, "You've got to work through what happened to you." Writing about my nightmares helped me get in touch with my past and reconnect with myself.* ~Cindy

What do you do if you wake up in the middle of the night and are scared to go back to sleep? What do you do if you have a recurring dream that frightens you? While you may feel powerless over your dreams, you are not. There is something you can do, and it's called imagery rehearsal.

## *Imagery Rehearsal Example*

Katelyn had a recurring dream for years. She dreamt a man was chasing her, and she could never see his face. The dream felt so real that she'd often wake up frightened, disoriented, and trembling in a cold sweat. She desperately wanted the dream to end, but didn't know how to make it stop.

It was during one of Katelyn's counseling sessions that she learned about imagery rehearsal, a technique to help with her recurring nightmare. Katelyn's therapist had her briefly describe her dream and then create a different ending: "Katelyn, you are the creator of your dream, so you can create a different ending. Remember that while some dreams may seem real, they are not predictors of the future. They are just images, thoughts, and sensations that occur during the sleep cycle."

Katelyn thought about how badly she wanted the dream to end. If she rewrote her dream, she would stop running, turn around, and face the man chasing her. She'd tell him, "STOP! Get out of my life once and for all!" The therapist told Katelyn to start imagining that ending a couple of times each day while she was awake. Before Katelyn left her session, she wrote down the new dream ending in a journal that she kept with her. She practiced the new ending over and over again. The first night Katelyn had the dream, she worked through the new ending and calmed herself more quickly than in the past. Over the course of a few weeks, to Katelyn's surprise, the nightmares began to subside and weren't as intense as in the past. Finally she was beginning to feel more rested and calmer before bed.

# directions

Conquer your nightmares by rewriting them. Answer the questions below to change your dream's ending.

1. Write down a nightmare that you continue to have or have had that bothers you.

   ______________________________________________

   ______________________________________________

   ______________________________________________

   ______________________________________________

   ______________________________________________

2. Like Katelyn, write an alternate ending to your dream. List ways you would change your nightmare. Remember you can change anything you want including characters, setting, time, and outcome.

   ______________________________________________

   ______________________________________________

   ______________________________________________

   ______________________________________________

3. Repeatedly practice your new ending for three to five minutes a couple of times per day. If the visions of your nightmare get too vivid, remind yourself it's just a dream.

4. Keep a copy of your new dream ending by your bedside. If you awaken from a nightmare, read the new ending out loud until you begin to calm down and relax.

## more to do

Take a look at sleep patterns that might be related to your nightmares. For example, do they occur when you lie on your back? Do they happen when you've had too much caffeine? Do they occur when you're overly exhausted? Once you identify your patterns, refer to activity 9 for some strategies to improve your overall sleep.

## words of inspiration

*Your nightmares are dreams, and while they may feel real, they aren't. They won't hurt you. Just like me, you too can overcome your nightmares and reclaim your life.* ~Cindy

# 22 coping with flashbacks

## you need to know

*Flashbacks* are sudden and vivid memories of a past traumatic event. They can be frightening, painful, and intrusive. A flashback can feel very real, as if the event is taking place in the current moment. Learning to ground yourself in the present moment can help you cope with intense flashbacks.

## my story

*It took me a couple of years before I started to heal. My faith played a large role in my healing process. I still can't remember every detail of the incident, but parts of it would play like a flashing disco light in my mind. I remember having recurring flashes of the incident, and they were frightening. When the flashbacks happened, it was my mind's way of bringing it up. I hadn't acknowledged or dealt with what happened. When I began to work through what happened, they started to go away, and now they don't interfere with my life.* ~Joi

Grounding is a technique that helps you put space between yourself and the flashback. It helps you focus on things in your environment while mindfully bringing you back to the present moment. Below are some examples of how to ground yourself and work through a flashback.

- Have special a trinket or memento that holds a fond memory within close reach (such as a piece of jewelry or a special picture). When you experience a flashback, grab hold of the item, focus on the positive memory associated with it, and connect yourself to the present moment. For example, *This is the special ring I got on my birthday. It is emerald green—the color of my birthstone. When I look at it, I will remember how old I am and focus on the fact that I am here, today, right now.*

- Study your environment. When a flashback is triggered, stop and pay close attention to your surroundings. Look at the colors and notice the patterns that are around you. For example, *I'm sitting on a red sofa, and the fabric is really soft; it feels like velvet. The floor is wood, and the grain patterns are all unique with waves and textures in each piece.*

- If you can, run water over your hands and pay attention to how the water feels as it's draining through the crevices between your fingers. Listen to the sound of the running water as it flows out of the faucet and lightly splashes in the basin. If you aren't near a faucet, find something you can do that involves your senses. Really focusing on different sensations can help you focus and stay calm.

- Play with your sense of taste. Pop a piece of gum or candy into your mouth. Focus on the intensity of the flavor.

# directions

Grounding techniques can be done any place and any time. Develop a plan to overcome flashbacks by responding to the prompts below.

1. When and where do your flashbacks occur?

_______________________________________________

_______________________________________________

_______________________________________________

_______________________________________________

_______________________________________________

2. What things trigger your flashbacks? For example, are there specific places you avoid driving by because they trigger a memory, does a particular song remind you of the past event, or is there a scent that takes you back to that moment in time?

_______________________________________________

_______________________________________________

_______________________________________________

_______________________________________________

_______________________________________________

_______________________________________________

3. List two to three grounding strategies from the list above that you will try the next time you experience a flashback.

_______________________________________________

_______________________________________________

_______________________________________________

4. Is there a special trinket or memento you can keep with you to help ground yourself should a flashback occur? For example, can you keep a smooth rock or marble in your pocket or a copy of your favorite inspirational poem in your wallet?

_______________________________________________

_______________________________________________

_______________________________________________

## more to do

The next time you experience a flashback, ground yourself in your five senses (seeing, hearing, smelling, touching, and tasting). In the space below, trace your hand. On each finger, write how you can use one of your senses to help bring you back to the present moment. In the palm, write down your favorite inspirational quote.

## words of inspiration

*Flashbacks can feel scary, but remember they are not real and you are safe.* ~Joi

# overcoming emotional detachment 23

## you need to know

Do you ever feel like you are watching someone else's life unfold before your eyes, only it's really yours? When you experience a traumatic event, it's hard to be in touch with your feelings, let alone express how you feel to others. In an effort to protect yourself, you may pull away from your feelings and relationships and become emotionally detached and numb.

## my story

*When it was happening, I mentally detached myself so I wouldn't feel the pain. While that helped me survive at fourteen, it became how I handled most every uncomfortable situation in my life for a long time. I thought being able to distance myself from the pain meant I was strong and "okay." I was living a lie, a horribly numb lie. It wasn't until I learned to be present in my body, mindful of my actions, and grateful for every moment that I realized I could release my past and truly live my life again.* ~Sidney

When you detach yourself from things you enjoy and pull away from the people you care about, you miss out on the good things that are happening around you. While detachment may provide a way to cope temporarily with the situation, it isn't a healthy long-term solution. Life is meant for living, and you can learn to reconnect and engage in living a more fulfilling life.

# directions

Despite how much you have been hurt, there is a part of you that wants to experience emotions and connect with the world. You don't have to walk through life feeling emotionally numb. While connecting with your feelings may feel frightening at first, you will be able to do it by taking small, manageable steps. Over time, it will become easier to express yourself and connect. You can show the world who you truly are.

1. What are some feelings you felt in the past that you miss feeling now?

   Example: *Joy*

   ________________________________________

2. What are some things that you have stopped doing that you once enjoyed?

   Example: *I stopped hanging around people because I felt insecure and frightened.*

   ________________________________________

   ________________________________________

   ________________________________________

3. Imagine having a magic wand and being able to make something you have pulled away from in life reappear. What would you make reappear?

   Example: *I would learn to have fun again. I would reconnect with my friends and let them get close to me again.*

   ________________________________________

   ________________________________________

   ________________________________________

# more to do

Your experience doesn't have to keep you detached from life. Learning to identify and express emotions can help you express yourself and deeply connect with others. Complete the statements below and add more if you need to.

I have trouble identifying the following emotions (for example, anger, sadness, or happiness):

_______________________________________________

_______________________________________________

_______________________________________________

I have trouble expressing the following emotions to others:

_______________________________________________

_______________________________________________

_______________________________________________

Emotional numbing keeps me from (for example, caring for other people):

_______________________________________________

_______________________________________________

Emotional numbing keeps me from: ________________________

_______________________________________________

Emotional numbing keeps me from: ________________________

_______________________________________________

Dream big and complete the statement below.

I wish I could *experience happiness when good things happen to me.*

I wish I could: ____________________________________________

____________________________________________

____________________________________________

Add three more:

1. ____________________________________________

____________________________________________

2. ____________________________________________

____________________________________________

3. ____________________________________________

____________________________________________

Now, take a look at the list, and rewrite each "I wish" statement as an "I will" statement. Part of your healing power will come from having the courage to connect with your emotions and with others. Every small step is powerful.

I wish I could *trust others again.*

I will *try to smile for a few seconds after something good happens, just as a reminder that it's okay to feel a few seconds of joy.*

I will... ______________________________

______________________________

______________________________

I will ______________________________

______________________________

I will ______________________________

______________________________

I will ______________________________

______________________________

Creating a specific plan, with specific behaviors, is the first step to achieving your dreams.

## words of inspiration

*When you feel like you have nothing to hold on to, stop, put your hand on your heart, and breathe deeply. Be in the moment. Look inward, and you will realize that you are your own strength.* ~Sidney

# 24 noticing and coping with anger

## you need to know

Anger is a common emotion that often emerges after experiencing sexual trauma. If handled appropriately, it can help you heal from your traumatic past. However, if used inappropriately, anger can hurt you and become destructive. Knowing your anger signs and managing them effectively can help you keep anger from getting out of control.

## my story

*Although sexual assault makes you feel powerless, you are not. Holding on to thoughts of anger and resentment is an easy thing to do, but doing so only hurts you. It's up to you to find a way to release your anger. Letting go of anger is a powerful and freeing act.*
~Amanda

Explore why you get angry. Is it because…

- no one seems to care about what happened to you?
- people you trusted failed to protect you?
- people blamed you for what happened?
- the justice system failed you?
- you didn't do something differently?

Although your angry thoughts may hold some truth and you have every right to be angry, there will come a time when you will have to decide what to do with your anger. Will you manage it or let it fester and grow? If you choose to manage it, recognizing signs from the three categories below will help.

## *1. Physical Cues*

When you get angry, your body gives off physical signs to let you know you're getting mad. The earlier you detect these signs, the quicker you can put strategies in place to calm down. Some of the physical cues your body may give when you're angry include:

- clenching your fists
- grinding your teeth
- rapid heartbeat
- flushed face
- sweating

When you feel your body responding to anger, you can leave the situation and decide to deal with it later. If that is not an option, you can take some deep, long, relaxing breaths and talk yourself through your anger.

Here is a script that you can use the next time you find your body responding to anger:

> Take a slow, deep breath and calm down. I can handle this situation. I just have to remain cool, calm, and collected.

## *2. Angry Thoughts*

Angry thoughts tell you that you're right and that what's happening isn't fair. Even when you have the right to be angry, these thoughts cloud your judgment. You can confront and cool a flaring temper by acknowledging your angry thoughts and learning to look at them from multiple perspectives. This is also known as challenging your thoughts.

Below are some examples of angry thoughts and ways to challenge them.

- *I can never trust anyone.* Acceptance and challenge: *Sure, there may be people I can't trust, but there are some I can. With time, I can learn how to figure out who can and cannot be trusted.*
- *What happened to me wasn't fair.* Acceptance and challenge: That is true. You can add "and" to this thought: *What happened to me wasn't fair, and I am going to find a way to overcome it.* That helps ease anger.
- *I feel other people think it was my fault.* Acceptance and challenge: Again there is a lot of victim blaming that happens after sexual trauma, and it isn't right. Learning to add *and that isn't right, and I don't have to let their feelings define me,* is another way to think about the situation.

If you get trapped in angry thoughts, even if they are justified, learning ways to accept and challenge them will help you feel better.

## *3. Angry Actions and Behaviors*

Anger can affect how you behave in situations. Below are some example of how anger affects what you say and how you act.

Angry actions include:

- interrupting people
- calling people names
- being overly bossy
- using unnecessary sarcasm
- cussing or swearing

Angry physical behaviors include:

- finger pointing
- hitting
- crying
- drinking too much
- overeating or undereating

## directions

How well do you know your anger signs? Identify your signs below.

1. **Physical cues:** What cues does your body give you when you are angry (for example, sweaty palms, heart racing, shaking)?

_______________________________________________

_______________________________________________

_______________________________________________

2. **Angry thoughts:** What are some examples of your angry thoughts (for example, *Everyone is against me, and I hate them*)?

_______________________________________________

_______________________________________________

_______________________________________________

3. **Angry actions and behaviors:** What are some things you've said (for example, "I don't care about anyone") or done (for example, swore at my friend, or refused to talk to anyone) to express anger?

| Things I've Said | Things I've Done |
|---|---|
| | |
| | |
| | |
| | |
| | |

## more to do

List some specific ways you can deal differently with your anger early in the process, when you first see the warning signs.

## words of inspiration

*It's true there are certain things that are outside of your control, but anger is in your control. Anger comes from within you. You can change how you respond to anger and overcome how it affects your life.* ~Amanda

# 25 constructive and destructive guilt

## you need to know

Many survivors struggle with the emotion "guilt." Guilt serves two very different and distinct purposes. First, it can be constructive and help you right a wrong. For example, if you purposefully hurt someone, cheated, or lied, constructive guilt tells you that you need to do something different in the future. Conversely, guilt can be destructive and make you feel responsible for something you had no control over. Understanding the purpose and reason behind guilt can help you cope with the uncomfortable emotion.

## my story

*I lay there crying, afraid to yell or to say "no" too harshly. What if he gets mad and leaves me stranded? Then I'd have to tell my mom I didn't really go to the mall and instead I went off to meet some boy she didn't even like. Maybe he will realize I don't want this and stop, I thought, but he didn't. Even though I didn't tell my mom, she still found out. Rather than supporting me, she seemed to care more that I couldn't wear white on my wedding day and about the embarrassment this would bring to the family. So I was left with an immense sense of guilt. I felt guilt for not fighting harder, for lying to my mother, and for disgracing my family. But wait, I was fourteen, I was raped, and it wasn't my fault. I had nothing to feel guilty about and neither do you.* ~Sidney

There are two types of guilt, constructive and destructive, and they have two very different roles in your life.

## Constructive Guilt

Constructive guilt is like a moral compass that tries to steer you in the right direction. It appears when you have wronged someone or done something that you shouldn't have done. It tells you, "You could've handled that in a better way," or "How would you like for someone to do that to you?" Constructive guilt helps guide you toward doing the right thing.

## Destructive Guilt

Destructive guilt does not steer you in the right direction, nor does it give you specific suggestions about how you can do better in the future. Instead, it tells you lies and takes situations that are beyond your control and blames you for them. Unfortunately, you may hear other people blame victims for their own trauma. These false, stereotyped beliefs are called "rape myths," and they are out there—in the media, in the courts, and even with friends. This makes it hard not to take in some of those hurtful messages, but if you can learn to identify them, you can fight back against destructive guilt.

In reality, you are responsible for only one person's actions: yours. What other people do is not your fault. If you are having trouble figuring out if you should feel guilty for something related to your sexual trauma, try to think of it this way: if someone were violated in a different way (say she was robbed or beaten up by a stranger), would you blame her for the situation? Although you want to try to stay safe and healthy, make sure you are not taking responsibility for things that are the perpetrator's fault. No one has the right to sexually violate another person, no matter what the circumstances.

# directions

Look at the statements below and identify whether the guilt is constructive or destructive. Write C for constructive or D for destructive next to each.

______ 1. I shouldn't have lied to my best friend about why I was late to our study group.

______ 2. I feel bad I reported what happened because he was arrested.

______ 3. If I hadn't been out so late, someone could have protected me from being assaulted.

______ 4. Because I got drunk at the party, he had the right to rape me.

______ 5. If I would have locked the door, it wouldn't have happened.

______ 6. If I would have said no, he wouldn't have continued hurting me.

______ 7. If I would have listened to my parents, they wouldn't have split up.

______ 8. If I would have worn a less revealing outfit, it wouldn't have happened.

______ 9. I shouldn't have made fun of that person because he probably felt bad afterward.

______ 10. If I hadn't been driving so fast, I wouldn't have gotten the speeding ticket.

## Answer Key

C = 1, 9, 10

D = 2, 3, 4, 5, 6, 7, 8

1. Which of the guilt statements in the list do you identify with?

___

___

___

2. List some of the guilt messages you give yourself.

___

___

___

___

3. Identify whether each guilt message you wrote is serving a constructive or destructive purpose.

___

___

___

___

___

# more to do

You can practice letting go of destructive guilt by letting it fade out of your life. Use the example below to watch this happen before your eyes.

You will need the following:

- slips of paper
- washable markers
- a container of water

On each slip of paper, write your destructive guilt messages. Reflect for a moment on one of your messages. Next, close your eyes and imagine letting the destructive guilt fade from your life. Open your eyes and drop the slip of paper into the container of water. Watch as the destructive guilt disappears. Repeat this exercise for each guilt message. Once your guilt has faded, take a deep breath and imagine the guilt being washed away from your life.

# words of inspiration

*Don't let guilt manipulate and deceive you into believing something that isn't true. It's not your fault, it never was, and it never will be. When guilt creeps in, remember that you did what you had to do to survive. And survive, you did.* ~Sidney

# conquering shame 26

## you need to know

Shame is a painful emotion that is often at the core of all sexual abuse. It is the burdensome feeling of being unworthy, humiliated, and unloved. Unlike guilt, in which you believe you did something bad, shame tells you that you are bad. Shame is about who you think you are.

## my story

> *I was assaulted many times in my life by people whom I was supposed to trust. I felt so ashamed and embarrassed. These people changed the course of my life, but they didn't take my life away from me. I had to learn how to live life by working through my shame and embarrassment. Working through my emotions was a learning experience. In my journey, I became a confident woman who found my voice. My voice gave me power, and that power told me I was good, I was strong, and I was a fighter.* ~Olivia

It's important to remember that sexual trauma violates everything you may have believed about the world. At our core, most of us would like to think bad things never happen to good people, or we'd like to think the world is predictable. Because sexual trauma violates our basic beliefs about the world, people sometimes blame the victim as a way to try to make sense of the situation. Unfortunately, that means that other people can also add to your shame. There is no way around it: a big part of healing is overcoming our shame-based thoughts—dealing with thoughts we might be telling ourselves or what we hear from those around us.

You can overcome and conquer shame by identifying the intent behind your shame-based thoughts and challenging them with more accurate ones.

You can identify the intent behind your thoughts by asking, "What is this thought trying to accomplish?" Shame-based thoughts are not productive thoughts; rather they can destroy your sense of security and confidence. Once you identify the purpose behind your shame-based thoughts, the next step is to challenge them.

How to challenge shame-based thoughts:

1. Look at the pros and cons of your thought. If the cons outweigh the pros, then challenge the shameful thought.

2. Examine whether your shame-based thoughts are accurate. For example, is it accurate to say "everyone" thinks negatively about you, or is it more accurate to say you feel that a lot of people don't think kindly of you?

3. Ask yourself, "What would I say to a friend in a similar situation?"

Here are some examples of shame-based thoughts, their purpose, and how to challenge them.

## Example 1

Shame-based thought: *I feel like a dirty person because this happened to me.*

Purpose: *To make me feel that what happened to me makes me a bad person.*

Challenge: *I did not choose to have this happen to me. He was responsible for this, and what happened to me doesn't make me a bad person.*

Example 2

**Shame-based thought:** I am a bad person because I didn't try to fight him off.

**Purpose:** To make me feel weak and vulnerable and that it was all my fault.

**Challenge:** It wasn't my fault. I did what I had to do to survive so that he didn't hurt me even more.

Example 3

**Shame-based thought:** I feel ashamed for not saying anything because he did it to someone else.

**Purpose:** To make me feel guilty and responsible for something I didn't do.

**Challenge:** It wasn't my fault. I was scared and didn't think anyone would believe me. I did the best I could to take care of myself.

# directions

Take a look at the shame-based thoughts below, identify their purpose, and challenge them like the examples above.

Shame-based thought: *I deserved what happened to me because I snuck out of the house the night it happened.*

Purpose: ______________________________________________

______________________________________________

______________________________________________

Challenge: ______________________________________________

______________________________________________

______________________________________________

Shame-based thought: *I feel there must be something about me that seems weak because my aunt said I invited this to happen to me.*

Purpose: ______________________________________________

______________________________________________

______________________________________________

Challenge: ______________________________________________

______________________________________________

______________________________________________

List three shame-based thoughts that you have. Identify their purpose and confront them with more accurate statements.

Shame-based thought: ______________________________________________

________________________________________________________________

________________________________________________________________

Purpose: ________________________________________________________

________________________________________________________________

________________________________________________________________

Challenge: ______________________________________________________

________________________________________________________________

________________________________________________________________

Shame-based thought: ______________________________________________

________________________________________________________________

________________________________________________________________

Purpose: ________________________________________________________

________________________________________________________________

________________________________________________________________

Challenge: ______________________________________________________

________________________________________________________________

________________________________________________________________

Shame-based thought: ____________________________________________

____________________________________________________________

____________________________________________________________

Purpose: ____________________________________________________

____________________________________________________________

____________________________________________________________

Challenge: __________________________________________________

____________________________________________________________

____________________________________________________________

# more to do

Carrying around the weight of shame can feel burdensome and heavy. It can take a toll on you both physically and mentally. By using visualization and metaphors, you can learn to release the hold shame has on your life. Give it a try: Get three small stones. Each stone represents one of the shame-based thoughts you listed above. Take your stones to a water source, such as a stream or pond, or fill a sink or tub with water.

Imagine each stone carrying the weight of the shame you feel. For each of your shame-based thoughts say:

> "I am not responsible for [insert shame-based thought], so I am releasing the weight of shame."

Drop the stone into the water. Imagine the weight of shame leaving your body and mind as the rock sinks into the depths of the water. Take a deep, cleansing breath as the stone's weight pulls it to the bottom. Repeat this sequence for each shame-based thought. After you drop the last stone, wrap your arms around yourself and give yourself a big hug—you deserve one!

# words of inspiration

> *You have no reason to feel ashamed and embarrassed. The person who assaulted you was in the wrong; he or she took your choice away from you. You had no control over what happened to you. You did nothing, absolutely nothing wrong.* ~Olivia

# 27 identifying depression

## you need to know

*Depression* is the persistent feeling of deep sadness. Many survivors of sexual trauma struggle with symptoms of depression. The good news is you can use various techniques to help you manage feelings of depression and boost your mood.

## my story

*I suffered from major depression. I could not cope with my past on my own, so I sought professional help and took prescribed medication to help me get through the dark times. Along with professional help, there were other rays of light in my life. I called them my seeds of hope. They were people who helped me get through the darkness and pain. It wasn't easy, but I was able to get through some really hard times and overcome my depression.* ~Cindy

Everyone gets down in the dumps, and some people bounce back quicker than others. The difference between depression and sadness is depression lasts longer and the feelings are usually more intense. Symptoms of depression can linger for days, weeks, and even months. They interfere with everyday functioning, making it difficult to concentrate, and keep you from being motivated. When depression starts to disrupt your life, then it's a signal to get immediate help.

# directions

Review the depression symptom checklist and check any symptoms you currently experience.

## Depression Symptom Checklist

- ☐ Sadness
- ☐ Helplessness
- ☐ Hopelessness
- ☐ Worthless or feeling guilty
- ☐ Bouts of crying
- ☐ Difficulty concentrating
- ☐ Forgetfulness
- ☐ Isolation
- ☐ Difficulty sleeping (too much or not enough)
- ☐ Loss of interest in activities and hobbies
- ☐ Fatigue
- ☐ Impulsivity
- ☐ Restlessness
- ☐ Irritability
- ☐ Aggressiveness
- ☐ Poor hygiene
- ☐ Poor appetite
- ☐ Weight changes (loss or gain)
- ☐ Self-harming behaviors
- ☐ Preoccupation with death

Answer the following questions:

1. Are there any other symptoms not listed that you currently experience?

______________________________________________________________

______________________________________________________________

______________________________________________________________

2. Which symptoms cause you discomfort?

______________________________________________________________

______________________________________________________________

______________________________________________________________

3. Are these symptoms interfering with your personal relationships or your ability to participate in school or work?

______________________________________________________________

______________________________________________________________

______________________________________________________________

Depression is treatable. If you are experiencing any of the symptoms above, you should talk to a trusted adult. You can figure out if someone is trustworthy by thinking about how he or she has supported you in the past. Has she been kind to you? Is he a good listener? For some people, it may feel like a challenge, but try to find people who care about you. When looking for support, think about the adults you know—parents, parents of your friends, school counselors, coaches, and teachers. If you have thoughts of hurting yourself, please seek help immediately.

# more to do

When you experience symptoms of depression, it's easy to withdraw and isolate yourself from others, but doing so will only make you feel worse. One way to deal with depression is to promise yourself that you will do something that you enjoy every day. Here are some examples:

- Watch a funny movie.
- Have lunch with a friend.
- Volunteer at a local animal shelter.
- Get your groove on and dance around the house.
- Go for a bike ride.
- Take a class to learn a new skill, such as sign language, cake decorating, pottery, or sewing.
- Join a book club.
- Learn a new sport like fencing, kickboxing, or rock climbing.

If you need more help, there are some wonderful resources in your community (check with your therapist or physician) and online that can give you ways to cope with depressed feelings.

Create your own list of mood boosters and use them the next time you experience symptoms of depression.

**Mood Booster List**

| | | |
|---|---|---|
| | | |
| | | |
| | | |
| | | |
| | | |

# words of inspiration

*Don't give up hope. It does get better. You will get through this moment in time, no matter how dark it feels. There is light at the end of the tunnel. There are people there for you, people who care and people who love you.* ~Cindy

# PTSD 28

## you need to know

*Post-traumatic stress disorder* (PTSD) is a set of symptoms that can happen months or even years after you experience sexual trauma. Although PTSD symptoms can feel scary and overwhelming, understanding the symptoms can help you cope with your feelings and emotions and decide if you need more help.

## my story

*As a child, I remember a psychologist telling me that I'm going to need to face what happened because if I don't, it will cause trouble later. I wish I would've listened, but instead I suppressed what happened, and it came back in the form of PTSD. I experienced symptoms of extreme panic attacks, flashbacks, and disturbing nightmares. The one thing I learned from my experience is not to block my emotions and to work through them no matter how painful it may be. You'll recover a lot quicker if you do.* ~Taylor

Symptoms of PTSD usually fall into four areas.

## 1. Re-experiencing Symptoms

These symptoms involve the feeling that the event is happening again. Symptoms include

- flashbacks
- nightmares
- intense distress when exposed to sights, sounds, or smells that remind you of the trauma
- intense bodily reactions when you recall the trauma

## 2. Avoidance Symptoms

These symptoms involve avoiding and blocking out anything that reminds you of the traumatic event. Symptoms include

- avoiding places, objects, and events that remind you of the event
- avoiding trauma-related thoughts and feelings

## 3. Difficult Thoughts and Moods

Symptoms include

- difficulty recalling things about the trauma
- negative and hopeless beliefs about the world and your future.
- self-blame or blame of others (who are not at fault)
- loss of interest in things you enjoyed before the trauma
- feeling isolated
- difficulty experiencing positive emotions

### 4. Reactivity

This involves feeling on guard and on edge. Symptoms include

- irritability or aggressiveness
- self-destructive behavior
- always aware and afraid of your environment
- easily startled
- difficulty concentrating
- trouble sleeping

You may also feel disconnected or dissociated from your body, as if you are in a dream or things around you are not real.

While it's completely normal to experience some of these symptoms in the first few weeks and months after a traumatic event, problems arise when the symptoms don't subside. These symptoms can impair your life. When trauma happens over months and years, these symptoms may become a constant way of coping.

# directions

Read the symptoms and answer yes or no to the questions. Then rate the amount of distress each symptom causes in your life, with 1 being minimal distress and 10 being maximum distress.

| PTSD Symptoms | Yes or No | Amount of Distress Symptom Causes in Your Life (1 = minimal distress, 10 = maximum distress) |
|---|---|---|
| Re-experiencing Symptoms | | |
| Do you ever feel as if the trauma is happening again? | | |
| Do you get easily upset when you are around people or places that remind you of the event? | | |
| Do you experience persistent and intense memories about the trauma? | | |
| Do you experience nightmares? | | |
| Do you experience bodily sensations, such as sweating, hot flashes, racing heart, or stomach pains, when you are reminded of the trauma? | | |
| Do you ever feel like you are "not yourself" or disconnected from your body when you are upset about the traumatic event? | | |

| | | |
|---|---|---|
| Avoidance Symptoms | | |
| Do you intentionally avoid certain places or situations that remind you of the event? | | |
| Do you avoid talking about the event? | | |
| Do you try to avoid thinking about the event? | | |
| Difficult Thoughts and Moods | | |
| Do you have trouble recalling the trauma, even when you try? | | |
| Do you feel hopeless about the future? | | |
| Do you continuously blame yourself or others for what they did to cause your trauma even though they are not at fault? | | |
| Have you lost interest in things you used to enjoy before the trauma happened? | | |
| Do you experience feelings of intense guilt or shame? | | |
| Do you have difficulty experiencing positive emotions, such as love, joy, and happiness? | | |

| PTSD Symptoms | Yes or No | Amount of Distress Symptom Causes in Your Life (1 = minimal distress, 10 = maximum distress) |
|---|---|---|
| Reactivity | | |
| Do you feel irritable most of the time? | | |
| Do you ever drink, smoke, cut yourself, or engage in risky sex to deal with your feelings? | | |
| Are you always scanning your environment for possible threats? | | |
| Are you easily startled? | | |
| Do you have difficulty concentrating? | | |
| Do you have trouble falling or staying asleep? | | |

If any of the symptoms above are causing you moderate to severe distress, please speak with a trusted adult to find a professional who can help you (see exercise 2 for ways to find an adult you can trust).

# more to do

Resilience is the ability to bounce back after something bad has happened. Building resilience is an important part of the recovery process. You can build resiliency by developing an action plan to put in place when you feel overwhelmed. Here are some examples:

- Reach out and talk to a friend about your troubles.
- Ask a trusted adult for help.
- Practice imagery or grounding skills.
- Find a peaceful place and take your self-soothing kit with you.
- Practice muscle relaxation techniques.
- Write in a journal.
- Engage in an enjoyable hobby, activity, or sport.
- Seek counseling from a mental health professional.

The next time you feel one of the symptoms you identified above, make a plan for how you can deal with that feeling. Use some of the resilience skills in your plan.

Dealing with Feelings

| What I Can Do: |
|---|
| 1. |
| 2. |
| 3. |
| 4. |
| 5. |

## words of inspiration

*Don't block out your emotions; they will resurface. Get professional help and know you aren't going to feel this way forever. This too will pass.* ~Taylor

# facing your fears 29

## you need to know

Fear is often triggered by specific people or things that are reminders of traumatic experiences. Fear causes physical, mental, and behavioral reactions that can lead to avoidance and isolation. Fear does not need to keep you from enjoying life. You can learn to face it and overcome its powerful grip.

## my story

*Right after the incident, I felt as if I lost all sense of safety. I was afraid he would come back or someone else would come after me. I experienced a level of fear most people never will. You know the feeling after you watch a scary movie when you're afraid to open the blinds, the closet, or the shower curtain because of the anxious feeling someone will be there, but you know no one is? In my situation, someone was there, and it took a while to work through my fear and anxiety. I had to come to a decision that I could spend the rest of my life living in fear or live my life. I made the difficult and conscious decision to face my fear and live my life.* ~Regan

While facing your fear can be scary at first, once you confront it, you'll realize it is not as scary as it feels. Here are some tools to help you face your fears:

1. Identify your specific fears. For example, are you afraid of the dark, being alone, dating, or crowded places?
2. Understand what your fear is doing to your body. For example, does it make your heart race, or do your palms start to sweat?

3. Understand what your fear tells you mentally. For example, does it tell you you'll never get through this or that you are unlovable?
4. Understand how your fear changes your behavior. Does it keep you from doing things you enjoy or make you feel that you can't trust anyone?
5. Determine whether or not your fear is realistic. Ask yourself these questions to see if you can think about your fears differently:
    - Would others think my fear is 100 percent true?
    - What would I say if someone described this situation to me?
    - Is there evidence that supports my fears?

# directions

Understanding and mentally challenging your fears is the first step in overcoming them. Answer the following questions.

| Understanding Your Fears | Your Answers |
|---|---|
| 1. Describe your fears. Are you afraid of specific places, certain people, or particular situations?<br>Example: *I am afraid of going places where there are lots of people.* | |
| 2. What does fear do to your body?<br>Example: *When I am in crowded places, I feel like I am going to have a heart attack. My heart races, and I break into a cold sweat.* | |
| 3. How does your fear affect your behavior?<br>Example: *I avoid going anywhere and live my life like a hermit. I am not very happy living my life locked in my house.* | |
| 4. What does your fear tell you about yourself and world around you?<br>Example: *My fear tells me to trust no one because someone will hurt me. I feel that I am unlovable because I am damaged.* | |

| Mentally Challenge Your Fears | Your Answers |
|---|---|
| 5. Look at what your fear is telling you about yourself and the world. Are the statements 100 percent true? Are there other ways to think about your fears?<br><br>Example: *My friend Sara would help me. I can trust her to stick by me in new and crowded places. I also know if I met someone who had been hurt, I wouldn't love him any less. Maybe I can get over this, not right away, but in time.* | |

## more to do

How is your fear limiting you? When you learn to face your fears in small, manageable steps, it's not nearly as scary as when you run from them. Build your courage by making a copy or taking a screenshot of the challenge you wrote above and use it the next time you feel afraid.

## words of inspiration

*Don't let your fear define who you are. You control your life and destiny.* ~Regan

# 30 identifying anxious patterns

## you need to know

Anxiety is an overwhelming emotion that can affect you in many different ways. It is completely normal to feel anxious at times, but when anxiety starts to limit daily routines, it can become problematic. You can ease your anxiety by understanding your symptoms and anxiety patterns and practicing healthy coping skills.

## my story

*I had extreme anxiety. Not only was I anxious and scared, but I also began to question my self-worth. My self-esteem and confidence were at an all-time low. Then I realized, I couldn't live like that anymore. I had to pull myself together. I decided I was going to beat the odds and be strong. I wasn't going to let the men who did this to me win. I also wasn't going to let my anxiety win. Once I made the decision to take back control of my life, my anxiety began to go away.* ~Olivia

Anxiety not only affects you emotionally and physically, but it also changes the way you act. Below are some examples of how anxiety can change your whole way of feeling, thinking, and behaving.

## 1. Emotions: What You Feel

Anxiety can cause different emotions to surface, including

- agitation
- indecisiveness
- panic
- restlessness
- stress
- worry

## 2. Thoughts: What You Think

Anxiety can lead you to

- jump to inaccurate conclusions
- make situations feel more serious than they really are
- think things will end with the worst-case scenario

## 3. Physical Responses: What Your Body Does

Anxiety can result in

- rapid heartbeat
- difficulty breathing
- sweating
- light-headedness
- headaches
- stomach problems

4. Behavioral Responses: What You Do

When you feel anxious, it's natural to try to fix the situation. Sometimes the things that you do will be healthy and positive (such as therapy, talking to friends, and yoga), and sometimes they may be unhealthy (such as self-injury or taking drugs). If you respond to anxiety in harmful ways, it can have long-lasting consequences. One of the best ways to deal with anxiety is to build healthier coping skills into your daily routine. Here are some examples:

- Talk to someone you trust.
- Engage in a hobby that helps to distract you.
- Use relaxation skills, such as guided imagery or yoga.
- Practice mindful breathing.
- Repeat encouraging thoughts, such as *I can handle this,* or *I will not feel this way forever.*

# directions

For the next week, keep a record of your anxiety symptoms to better understand how anxiety is affecting your daily life. Tracking your symptoms will also let you see how well you are managing your anxious feelings.

| Anxiety-Provoking Situation | Anxious Emotions | Anxious Thoughts | Physical Responses to Anxious Thoughts | Behavioral Responses |
|---|---|---|---|---|
| **Example:** Sitting in a crowded movie theater. | What if I can't breathe and I panic? | I need to get out of the theater. Don't go back; you'll never be able to go back. | Felt dizzy, nauseous, and as if my heart was beating out of my chest. | Left the theater to get some fresh air and sat in the car until the movie was over. |
| | | | | |
| | | | | |
| | | | | |
| | | | | |
| | | | | |

# more to do

Once you've made a few entries, use your responses to answer the following prompts.

1. Are there any particular times of the day when your anxiety occurs most often (for example, in the evening when you are tired or in the morning when you first wake up)?

2. List any common symptoms you felt when you became anxious.

3. List any patterns that you saw emerge when you became anxious.

_______________________________________________

_______________________________________________

_______________________________________________

_______________________________________________

_______________________________________________

4. Based on your patterns (the time of day you feel most anxious, or specific situations that make you anxious), list three healthy coping strategies that you can use to deal with anxiety.

_______________________________________________

_______________________________________________

_______________________________________________

_______________________________________________

_______________________________________________

## words of inspiration

*You can't spend your life anxious and worrying about the issues, problems, and situations that you can't control. Why worry about the future? You can't change what hasn't happened. Why worry about the past? You can't change what has already happened. You can only change the things that are in your control to change.* ~Olivia

# 31 responding to love and joy

## you need to know

Learning to experience positive emotions is an important part of recovery. Survivors of sexual trauma may feel they are unworthy of love and joy. Perhaps they believe that if they allow themselves to feel happiness, something bad will happen. However, not allowing themselves a chance to experience these positive emotions can keep them from living life to its fullest.

## my story

*I learned to love again when I stopped faulting myself for what someone else did to me. I learned that not everyone is out to hurt me. Knowing that I am deserving and worthy of love helps me hold myself in high regard. I had to learn to find joy in life and love myself. And, yes it can get lonely, but you have to learn to love yourself, find joy in life, find comfort in doing things by yourself, and believe, whether you are with someone or not, you are going to be okay. When you love yourself enough, you won't allow anything else less than good to come into your life.* ~Tanisha

Love and joy are not tangible, meaning you can't see these emotions; you can only express and feel them. The words "I love you" are some of the strongest words known to humanity. Loving yourself is as important as loving other people, and it begins with developing healthy relationships, learning to feel worthy of respect, and allowing yourself to experience joy.

There are two fundamentals in learning to experience positive emotions, such as love and joy. First, you have to acknowledge when the feelings are present. If you have numbed yourself to your feelings, it will take time for your emotions to wake up, but they will awaken again. Second, you have to practice expressing love and joy, to both yourself and others.

# directions

Write down as many words as you can to describe "love" and "joy." If you are having trouble, use a dictionary or a search engine to help you find synonyms.

Over the course of a day, keep a list of any positive emotions you feel. Even if you experience something positive for a few seconds, write it down. Do this every day for a week.

After a week, look at your list. If you expressed those feelings to someone else, circle them. If you did not express those feelings to anyone, write a few sentences describing how you could have expressed those feelings to someone.

Example: *"Mom, the breakfast you made was really good. It was nice to hang out with you for a few minutes."*

_______________________________________________

_______________________________________________

_______________________________________________

_______________________________________________

_______________________________________________

# more to do

In order to find joy, you have to open your heart to love.

1. Inside the heart, write ways you can express love or joy to yourself. For example, list some things that you enjoy doing that help you feel love and happiness, such as:
   - spending time with someone you care about
   - walking in the park
   - playing with your beloved pet
2. Outside of the heart, write down the things that are keeping you from experiencing love and joy. For example, are you blaming yourself for the past, are you holding a grudge against someone, or are you protecting yourself from getting hurt?
3. The next time you desire love and joy, do some of the items you listed in your heart. By engaging in loving care toward yourself over time, you will be able to better express this emotion to others and to feel more joy in your life.

*Open Hearts*

## words of inspiration

*Be open to love and joy. Don't let your past hinder you from moving forward. Be open to getting to know new people and exploring new relationships.* ~Tanisha

# 32 empowerment through affirmations

## you need to know

*Empowerment* is the process of building yourself up and believing in your strength and abilities. One way to empower yourself is through affirmations. Affirmations are positive statements of truth that tell you that you are competent, smart, and worthy of being loved. Good affirmations aren't just general statements. They are actually tied to specific behaviors—things you do each day.

## my story

*I was sexually abused by someone I knew and trusted. I remember feeling confused, humiliated, and violated afterward. Because I had drank the night of the incident, I blamed myself and felt guilty for what happened. Then I began to realize it wasn't my fault. Why was I beating myself up? I realized I had to work on myself, and with the help of my faith and supportive friends, I did just that. I began change the way I treated and thought about myself. Rather than tearing myself down, I started to build myself up. I started believing in my abilities and encouraging myself to push forward. I started opening up and not shutting down. I started surrounding myself with positivity while omitting as many negatives that I could. Those actions made a huge difference in my healing process.* ~Paige

Composing affirmations is a skill that can be learned, but it is not easy. People have a tendency to beat themselves up if they fail at something or make poor choices. They tell themselves they will never fulfill their dreams.

When you constantly tell yourself you aren't good enough, aren't smart enough, or aren't worthy, you will feel mentally and physically drained. Fortunately, you can learn to change those nagging voices by challenging them and then focusing your attention on your accomplishments, however small. For example, you can say to yourself, "I am proud I was able to hand in my math assignment on time even though I had trouble sleeping," or "I give myself credit for talking to that cute guy, even though I felt really nervous." When you learn to think like this, you are gathering evidence to challenge those thinking patterns that put you down.

# directions

Affirmations are the building blocks to empowerment. Below are two walls: a self-defeating wall and an affirmation wall. On the self-defeating wall, write the unhelpful messages that cycle through your mind. On the affirmation wall, confront the self-defeating messages with helpful affirmations that are tied to something specific you've done.

| Self-Defeating Wall | Affirmation Wall |
|---|---|
| Example: No one likes me. | I talked to the new girl in my English class, and we had a nice conversation. |
| | |
| | |
| | |

Make copies of your affirmation wall and post them in accessible places (such as on your bathroom mirror, in your school notebook, or on your nightstand). Practice adding new statements every day. Remember, the key to success is giving yourself credit for your accomplishments, even if they seem small.

# more to do

Learning to use affirmations is like learning a new language. It won't come naturally, so practice and patience are very important. How you speak to yourself affects your life experiences. If you continue to focus on your daily successes, the negative voices will lose their power and fade into the background.

List three positive things, however small, that are currently happening in your life. Then, write about how you contributed to creating those positive situations.

Example: *I enjoy cooking. I decided it would be nice to bake cookies every week with my little sister, and I'm the one who asked her if we should do that. She seems to enjoy it.*

1. ______________________________

______________________________

______________________________

2. ______________________________

______________________________

______________________________

3. ______________________________

______________________________

______________________________

Once you begin to use affirmations to confront self-defeating messages, you will become more empowered and confident.

## words of inspiration

*First and foremost, remain strong and be true to yourself. It's easier said than done, but when you believe in who you are, you can find the strength to overcome any obstacle life throws your way.* ~Paige

# respecting and nurturing yourself 33

## you need to know

*Self-respect* is the acceptance of yourself as a person, regardless of your past. It involves treating yourself with honor and dignity and expecting others to treat you with the respect you deserve.

## my story

*I was raped, multiple times, and it wasn't my fault. I have learned to take ownership for everything I do in my life, but I won't take ownership of what happened to me. There is absolutely nothing I did that warranted ownership of the rape. The person who raped me tried to destroy me, but I didn't let him. Don't let the person who did this to you destroy you. What happened isn't your fault. Don't own something you didn't do. I had to learn to respect myself and move forward, and if I can find the strength to do it, so can you.*
~Tanisha

Through this journey you have blossomed into an amazing young woman. Take time to celebrate who you are and how far you have come. As you continue your journey, stay focused on treating yourself with dignity and high self-worth. You can begin respecting yourself by doing some of the following things.

* Focus on healthy ways to make yourself feel good and do them.
    - Exercise.
    - Talk to friends.
    - Engage in a hobby you enjoy, such as cooking or sports.
    - Practice your favorite distraction, such as listening to music.

* Use mindfulness skills to get back in touch with how you are feeling and what you are thinking in the present moment.
    - Breathe in and out slowly with one hand on your chest and one hand on your abdomen. See if you can get most of the air to flow into your abdomen.
    - Now, put one hand over your heart and breathe. Focus on how your mind feels calmer as your body slows down.
* Identify how you want to be treated by others and expect to be treated that way. If you are in a relationship in which you are not being treated with respect, consider changing that relationship.
    - Remember that people who respect you should never repeatedly put you down, call you names, or physically harm you.
    - People who respect you encourage you to grow, take time to listen to you, and value your thoughts and feelings.

## directions

How you see yourself, how you treat yourself, and how you allow others to treat you can become your reality and in turn affect your self-respect. Just as a flower needs nurturing to bloom into an amazing natural occurrence, you too will blossom into a strong and confident young woman with care and nurturing. It's time to show the world what you have to offer.

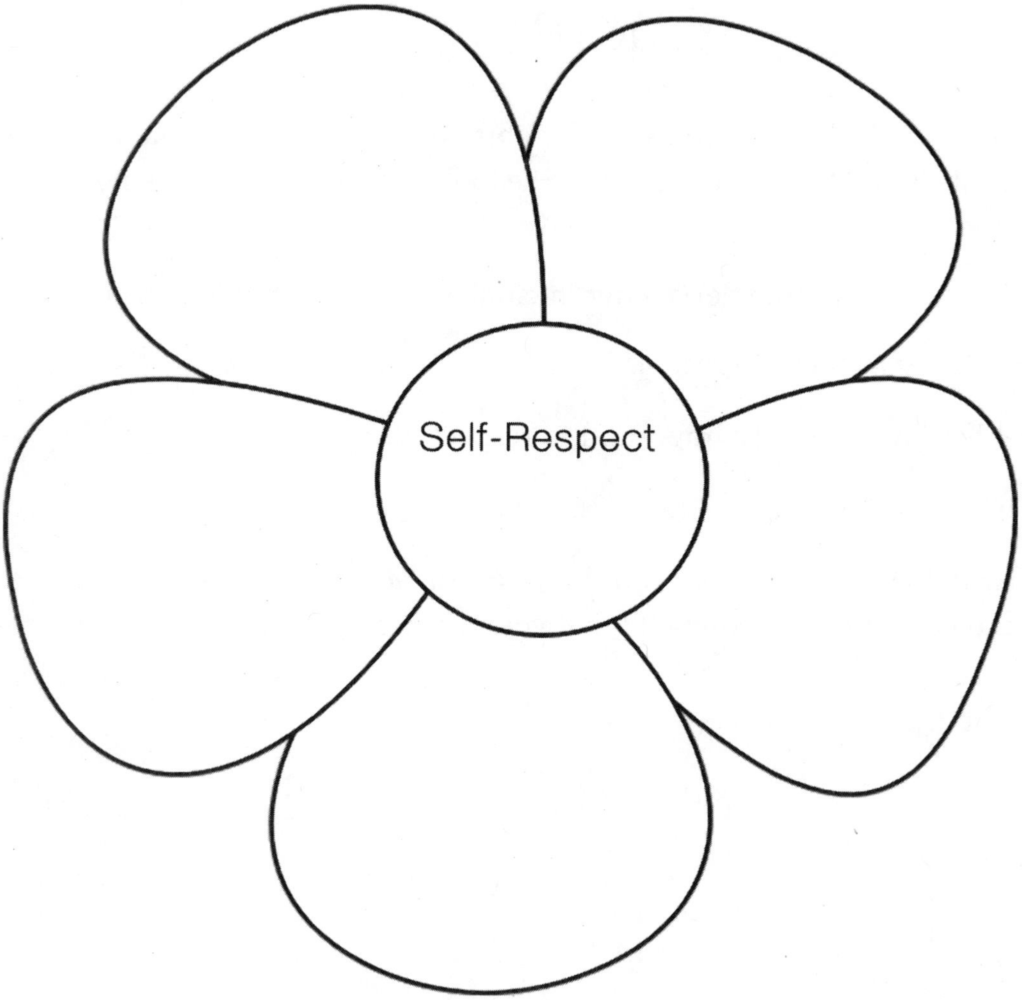


Using the three ways to develop self-respect we've described, complete the flower petals with the following information.

Write something that makes you feel good and you enjoy doing (two petals).

Write how you would like to be treated by others (one petal). Be as specific as possible. Examples: *I expect not to be hit, sworn at, or put down*, or *I'd like a friend who will listen when I'm upset and not just change the subject.*

Write things you can do to focus on your present thoughts and emotions (two petals). Examples: *Mindful breathing or visualization.*

# more to do

Imagine that a girl who has been sexually abused is approaching you. Her self-esteem is low, and she bows her head in shame. She looks up to you as a role model and needs your guidance.

Offer her advice by writing her a letter. Include the following items in your letter.

- Tell her what "self-respect" is.
- Let her know why it's important to respect oneself.
- Give her specific suggestions about how she can start respecting herself.

Remember the same advice you would give to someone else is the same advice you should take yourself. Give yourself what you deserve: love, compassion, and respect.

Dear ________________________________________,

______________________________________________________________________

______________________________________________________________________

______________________________________________________________________

______________________________________________________________________

______________________________________________________________________

______________________________________________________________________

______________________________________________________________________

______________________________________________________________________

______________________________________________________________________

______________________________________________________________________

______________________________________________________________________

______________________________________________________________________

______________________________________________________________________

## words of inspiration

*Respect yourself. Forgive yourself. Forgive the person who did this to you. Allow yourself freedom to move forward. Allow yourself time to heal. Time does heal.* ~Tanisha

# 34 from beginning to end—telling your story

## you need to know

No one's story is like yours. You began this journey by sharing a part of your story, and throughout this book, other women have shared parts of their story with you. From beginning to end, you have opened the chapters to your story and learned necessary skills to reclaim your life. Your story is one of a beautiful young woman who knows what it means to survive and thrive!

## our story

*From the onset of this book, we had one person in mind: you. We hope this book has helped you to find your way and given you hope to conquer life's mountains. Dealing with trauma doesn't make you a weak person; it makes you strong. You have nothing to be ashamed of; in fact, you should be proud. You are a survivor. May you continue to build confidence and find the strength to achieve your dreams. As we bring this book to a close, we want you to know your unyielding desire to push through difficult times makes you a remarkably strong and resilient young woman.* ~Raychelle and Sheela, the authors

Your story, your life, has a lot of wonderful things that await you. To quote the famous Dr. Seuss, "Oh, the places you'll go!" As each day passes, you write more and more in your book of life. Of course, what you have experienced will always be a part of your story. While you won't be able to take the traumatic experience out of your book, the rest of the story doesn't have to be defined by your past.

# directions

Complete the story and fill in the spaces with information that you have learned throughout this book. Feel free to flip back to prior activities and revisit your growth throughout this process.

Once upon a time, there was a girl named ______________________ (your name) who struggled with ___________________________. Over time, she realized she needed to take better care of herself by _________________________. She also learned she could cope by using ______________________ to help her get through life's difficult times. In order to work through her past, she had to explore unhelpful coping skills such as_____________________________ that interfered rather than helped with her recovery. Also she had to explore painful emotions including _____________________________________ to help her work through her past.

Fortunately, as time went on, she began to practice the skills to develop into a strong and courageous young woman. She learned to believe in her abilities and live in the moment. She found her voice and learned to respect herself by

_____________________________________________________________________.

This extraordinary young woman __________________________ (your name) has some wonderful dreams to fulfill including __________________. So, watch out world for ______________________________ (your name). *Oh, the places she will go!*

## more to do

In this book, more than fifteen women have written to you with personal words of inspiration. They wanted to help encourage you throughout your journey. At the beginning of the book, you wrote your own words of inspiration, but now you're in a different chapter of life. What words of inspiration would you like to provide to end this chapter?

My personal words of inspiration:

______________________________________________

______________________________________________

______________________________________________

______________________________________________

## words of inspiration

*From the bottom of our hearts, thank you for letting us be a part of your journey. You are an amazing young woman, and we are inspired by your courage and strength. It is our sincere wish that you will continue to grow personally and know you are a survivor! Wishing you all the best as you continue your journey.* ~ Raychelle and Sheela, the authors

# acknowledgments

We would like to thank Tesilya Hanauer for her insightful wisdom and guidance through the creation of this book. We sincerely appreciate her ability to connect two authors with similar passions so that we could bring this book into existence.

# additional resources

Reaching out for help is an important part in of the healing process, and there are a lot of great organizations devoted to providing support and guidance for sexual assault survivors. You can learn more about the services they provide by visiting their websites.

*The list of resources isn't an endorsement of any organization; rather it's a way to help you begin the search for reputable and supportive agencies.*

**Darkness to Light:** A nationwide agency dedicated to ending child sexual abuse.

http://www.d2l.org

**National Sexual Assault Hotline:** A nationwide hotline that provides free, confidential services 24/7 to anyone who has experienced sexual assault.

1–800–656-HOPE

**NSVRC (National Sexual Violence Resource Center):** A national agency that focuses on preventing and responding to sexual violence.

http://www.nsvrc.org

**RAINN (Rape, Abuse & Incest National Network):** The nation's largest anti-sexual violence organization. This agency can help locate local sexual abuse agencies as well as provides an online hotline for those who need immediate help.

http://www.rainn.org

**The Office on Women's Health:** A US governmental agency that works to improve the health and well-being of all women, whose "Violence Against Women" web page is especially helpful.

http://www.womenshealth.gov/violence-against-women

**Raychelle Cassada Lohmann, MS, LPC**, is a national board-certified counselor and licensed professional counselor. Lohmann has worked as a school counselor at middle and high school levels, and has helped hundreds of teens deal with feelings of frustration and anger. She has participated in extensive research on anger, and specializes in individual and group counseling for anger management. She is author of *The Anger Workbook for Teens* and *Staying Cool...When You're Steaming Mad*, and coauthor of *The Bullying Workbook for Teens*. She also writes the *Psychology Today* blog "Teen Angst," and is an expert contributor on www.rehabs.com and www.sharecare.com.

**Sheela Raja, PhD**, is a licensed clinical psychologist and author of *Overcoming Trauma and PTSD*. Raja is an assistant professor at the University of Illinois at Chicago, where she researches the impact of trauma on health. Raja completed internship and post-doctoral training at the National Center for PTSD in Boston, MA. She is a highly sought-after national and international speaker, a blogger for *The Huffington Post*, and a frequent contributor to various print and television media outlets.

# More Instant Help Books for Teens

An Imprint of New Harbinger Publications

**THE SELF-ESTEEM WORKBOOK FOR TEENS**

Activities to Help You Build Confidence & Achieve Your Goals

**ISBN: 978-1608825820 / US $15.95**

**THE ANXIETY WORKBOOK FOR TEENS**

Activities to Help You Deal with Anxiety & Worry

**US $14.95 / ISBN: 978-1572246034**

**THINK CONFIDENT, BE CONFIDENT FOR TEENS**

A Cognitive Therapy Guide to Overcoming Self-Doubt & Creating Unshakable Self-Esteem

**US $16.95 / ISBN: 978-1608821136**

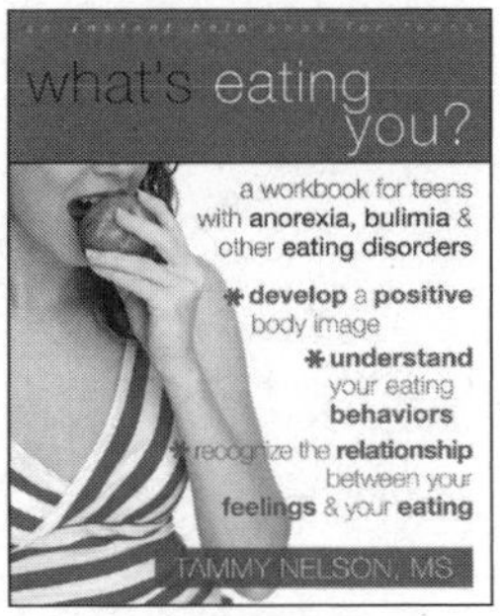


**WHAT'S EATING YOU?**

A Workbook for Teens with Anorexia, Bulimia & other Eating Disorders

**ISBN: 978-1572246072 / US $16.9**

**THE BODY IMAGE WORKBOOK FOR TEENS**

Activities to Help Girls Develop a Healthy Body Image in an Image-Obsessed World

**ISBN: 978-1626250185 / US $16.95**

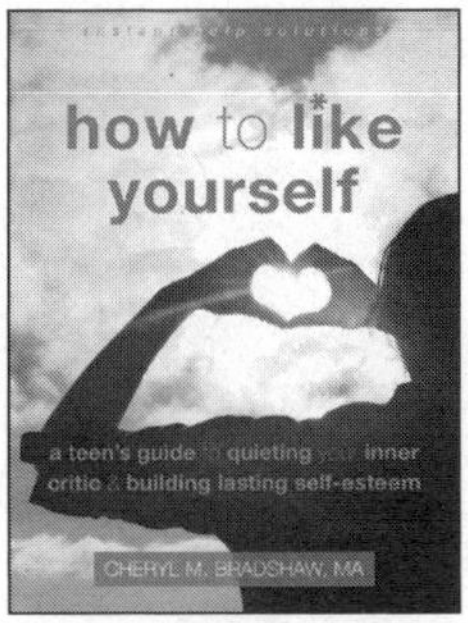


**HOW TO LIKE YOURSELF**

A Teen's Guide to Quieting Your Inner Critic & Building Lasting Self-Esteem

**ISBN: 978-1626253483 / US $16.95**

newharbingerpublications
1-800-748-6273 / newharbinger.com

(VISA, MC, AMEX / prices subject to change without notice)

Follow Us

Don't miss out on new books in the subjects that interest you.
Sign up for our **Book Alerts** at **newharbinger.com/bookalerts**

## ARE YOU SEEKING A CBT THERAPIST?

The Association for Behavioral & Cognitive Therapies (ABCT) Find-a-Therapist service offers a list of therapists schooled in CBT techniques. Therapists listed are licensed professionals who have met the membership requirements of ABCT & who have chosen to appear in the directory.

**Please visit www.abct.org & click on *Find a Therapist*.**

Register your **new harbinger** titles for additional benefits!

When you register your **new harbinger** title—purchased in any format, from any source—you get access to benefits like the following:

- Downloadable accessories like printable worksheets and extra content
- Instructional videos and audio files
- Information about updates, corrections, and new editions

Not every title has accessories, but we're adding new material all the time.

Access free accessories in 3 easy steps:

1. Sign in at NewHarbinger.com (or **register** to create an account).
2. Click on **register a book**. Search for your title and click the **register** button when it appears.
3. Click on the **book cover or title** to go to its details page. Click on **accessories** to view and access files.

That's all there is to it!

If you need help, visit:

NewHarbinger.com/accessories

new harbinger
CELEBRATING
40 YEARS